THE PSYCHOLOGICAL RESILIENCE TREATMENT MANUAL

The Psychological Resilience Treatment Manual (PRTM) provides mental health professionals with an evidence-based guide to psychological resilience treatment designed to equip clients with a toolbox of adaptive coping strategies.

This intervention treatment manual is for practitioners working with clients to develop resilience and the skills they need to cope with daily challenges, reduce stress levels, and increase general well-being without necessarily diagnosing a specific disorder, such as anxiety or depression. The manual is structured around four guided intervention modules: Passive Coping, Self-Care Behaviour, Social Support, and Active Coping. Each module encompasses four one-hour sessions and includes a contents framework, overview, and target objectives for each session. The manual includes 16 client worksheets that correspond to each session, and relapse prevention therapy is incorporated at the end of each module. Flexible in nature, the manual can be used by practitioners in its entirety or modules can be selected as appropriate, depending on a client's needs.

The Psychological Resilience Treatment Manual is an essential resource for qualified and registered psychologists, qualified cognitive behavioural therapy (CBT) practitioners, psychiatrists, and postgraduate counselling psychology students.

Saralla Chettiar is a PhD candidate at the School of Psychology at Massey University in New Zealand and a practising clinical psychologist in Malaysia. Her published works include reviewing a book on military stress and resilience. Her PhD initiative was cited as a highly commendable contribution to public health and safety at a conference in Edinburgh, Scotland, in 2019.

Ian de Terte, PhD, is a senior lecturer and clinical psychologist at the School of Psychology at Massey University in New Zealand. He has published over 50 articles and has been invited to present at local and international meetings on over 30 occasions on the subject of psychological resilience, coping strategies, and traumatic stress with high-risk or first-responder populations. Dr. de Terte is a former detective with the New Zealand Police and a reservist clinical psychologist with the New Zealand Defence Force.

THE PSYCHOLOGICAL RESILIENCE TREATMENT MANUAL

An Evidence-based Intervention Approach

Saralla Chettiar and
Ian de Terte

Routledge
Taylor & Francis Group

LONDON AND NEW YORK

Cover image: © Getty Images

First published 2022
by Routledge
4 Park Square, Milton Park, Abingdon, Oxon OX14 4RN

and by Routledge
605 Third Avenue, New York, NY 10158

Routledge is an imprint of the Taylor & Francis Group, an informa business

British Library Cataloguing-in-Publication Data
A catalogue record for this book is available from the British Library

Library of Congress Cataloging-in-Publication Data
Names: Chettiar, Saralla, author. | de Terte, Ian, author.
Title: The psychological resilience treatment manual : an evidence-based intervention /
    Saralla Chettiar, Ian de Terte.
Description: Abingdon, Oxon ; New York, NY : Routledge, 2022. |
    Includes bibliographical references and index.
Identifiers: LCCN 2021055429 (print) | LCCN 2021055430 (ebook) |
    ISBN 9781032188836 (hardback) | ISBN 9781032188812 (paperback) |
    ISBN 9781003256779 (ebook)
Subjects: LCSH: Resilience (Personality trait) | Adjustment (Psychology) |
    Evidence-based psychotherapy.
Classification: LCC BF698.35.R47 C44 2022 (print) | LCC BF698.35.R47 (ebook) |
    DDC 155.2/4–dc23/eng/20211115
LC record available at https://lccn.loc.gov/2021055429
LC ebook record available at https://lccn.loc.gov/2021055430

ISBN: 978-1-032-18883-6 (hbk)
ISBN: 978-1-032-18881-2 (pbk)
ISBN: 978-1-003-25677-9 (ebk)

DOI: 10.4324/9781003256779

Typeset in Stone Serif
by Apex CoVantage, LLC

I owe the foundation of everything that I am to my faith and family.
To my heart and soul, Clement and Nikita Pakiam, you hold my infinite love and gratitude.
My parents, Murugappa Chettiar and Teresa Andrews, who believed I could.

Saralla Chettiar

I dedicate this book to my parents. My mother passed away some years ago during my doctorate, and this research project commenced me on the path to resilience. My father passed away recently, when this book was coming to fruition. Without both of them, I would not be where I am today—thank you, mum and dad.

Ian de Terte

CONTENTS

List of figures ix
List of tables x
Acknowledgements xi

INTRODUCTION 1
Objective 1
Abstract and module overview 2
Disclaimer 3
Recommendations to mental health professionals 3

MODULE 1 Passive coping 6
Session 1: The psychology of coping and venting 8
Session 2: Reviewing behaviour disengagement and self-distraction activities 14
Session 3: Addressing self-blame and denial tendencies 20
Session 4: Metacognition and relapse prevention exercises 27
Appendix A: Client worksheets for passive coping module 32

MODULE 2 Self-care behaviours 47
Session 5: Getting active and proper nutrition—paying attention 50
Session 6: Mindfulness practice—all about thoughts, feelings, and body sensations 55
Session 7: Practising self-compassion techniques 59
Session 8: Learning how to relax, managing time, space, and meaning-making activities; revisiting relapse prevention exercises 63
Appendix B: Client worksheets for self-care module 68

MODULE 3 Social support 79
Session 9: Structural and functional social support 82
Session 10: Emotional social support 87
Session 11: Instrumental or material social support 89
Session 12: Information or cognitive social support and relapse prevention exercises 91
Appendix C: Client worksheets for social support module 94

MODULE 4 Active coping 98
Session 13: Introduction to active coping, stress experience, and reactions 101
Session 14: Positive reframing, tracking thoughts, behaviour, and learning effective problem-solving techniques 107

Session 15: Utilising restraint coping, grateful journaling, and relapse prevention
exercises   110
Session 16: Humour—an active coping strategy   114
Appendix D: Client worksheets for active coping module   119

Index   131

FIGURES

1.1	Modified operational model of stress and coping (passive coping)	10
1.2	Mood tracking graph	12
1.3	Schematic diagram of personal responsibility and behavioural disengagement in innocent bystanders during classroom management events	14
A1.1	Modified operational model of stress and coping (passive coping)	33
A1.2	Mood tracking graph	36
A1.3	Schematic diagram of personal responsibility and behavioural disengagement in innocent by standers during classroom management events	37
3.1	Individual's social support	83
4.1	Modified operational model of stress and coping (active coping)	103
4.2	Stages of stress reaction	105
4.3	Discrete thought tracking (DTT) and action plan activity	108
4.4	Types of humour	115
A4.1	Modified operational model of stress and coping (active coping)	120
A4.2	Stages of stress reaction	122
A4.3	Discrete thought tracking (DTT) and action plan	123

TABLES

1.1	Tracking personal responsibilities and goal achievements	17
1.2	Red flags for behaviour disengagement	18
1.3	Managing and tracking behaviours that lead to setback	19
1.4	Attention: Self-focus and others-focus	23
1.5	Tracking anticipatory worry, mind-reading, and post-analysis thoughts	23
A1.1	Managing venting behaviour	35
A1.2	Red flags for behaviour disengagement	40
A1.3	Handling setbacks	40
A1.4	Tracking attention	41
A1.5	Tracking thoughts	42
A1.6	Tracking behaviours	42
2.1	Benefits of exercising for physical and mental health	50
2.2	Good nutrition for mental and physical health	50
2.3	Typical and nontypical exercise options	51
2.4	Important reminders for effective diet and cooking plans	51
2.5	Informal mindfulness practice check-ins	56
2.6	Compassionate note, statement to self, or positive self-talk log-ins	61
2.7	Self-care activities—managing time and space	64
2.8	Meaning-making activities	64
A2.1	Benefits of exercising for physical and mental health	69
A2.2	Good nutrition for mental and physical health	69
A2.4	Important reminders for effective diet and cooking plans	69
A2.5	Informal mindfulness practice check-ins	71
A2.6	Compassionate note, statement to self, or positive self-talk log-ins	73
A2.7	Self-care activities—managing time and space	75
A2.8	Meaning-making activities	76
3.1	Conservation of Resources (COR) theory	82
A3.1	Conservation of Resources (COR) theory	95
4.1	Restraint coping exercises	111
A4.1	Restraint coping exercises	125

ACKNOWLEDGEMENTS

I would like to begin by expressing my utmost gratitude to the School of Psychology, Department of Humanities and Social Sciences, Massey University, Wellington, New Zealand in allowing me to pursue my PhD goals. In doing so, they allowed me to transform my clinical experiences into a treatment manual. The ultimate goal was always to provide mental health professionals with access to evidence-based psychological resilience interventions packed with adaptive coping strategies for the benefit and well-being of clients.

My appreciation and thanks to my main supervisor and coauthor, Dr. Ian de Terte, Senior Lecturer and Clinical Psychologist, who helped me fine-tune my ideas into polished products and mentored me in building the structure of this treatment manual. Thanks also to Dr. Melissa de Wolff, Senior Clinical Psychologist and Clinic Director of Massey Psychology Clinic, and to Dr. Simon Bennett, Director of Clinical Psychology programme, Wellington, who both provided space, opportunity, and gracious support in allowing this treatment manual to reach its pinnacle of efficacy.

To the administrative support team—Megan Burnett, Claire Grant (Department of Humanities and Social Sciences, Massey University, Wellington), and Carrie Wilson (Massey Psychology Clinic, Wellington)—my heartfelt thanks and immense gratitude for the support rendered in various ways during the development and testing of this treatment manual.

To my postgraduate mates and colleagues, Dr. John B. Guilaran, George Guthrie, Dr. Alexia Sweet, and Daniella Zhao, who made me miss home a little less.

Finally, my immense gratitude to my husband, Clement, for his love, respect, and trust in supporting me to be the best version of myself at any point of time. His editorial support and unwavering belief in me have made this mission that much more possible.

Saralla Chettiar

INTRODUCTION

Manualised treatment interventions are intended to support mental health professionals in providing effective treatment sessions to clients. Utilising tailor-made evidence-based treatment intervention manuals allows mental health professionals to build efficient therapeutic interactions, implement effective interventions, and obtain improved outcomes from their clients.

Commonly observed outpatient referral categories include individuals who have experience cumulative stress, trauma, inappropriate coping skills, and anxiety-related symptoms. Practising effective coping styles, self-care behaviours, and learning how to find adequate social support are effective ways to reduce daily stress and increase general well-being in these individuals. Focused, evidence-based treatment interventions found in this manual can promote learning of these skills in a structured manner.

(PRTM) aims to offer evidence-based interventions for mental health professionals. Clinical psychologists, psychiatrists, and other cognitive behavioural therapy (CBT)-trained mental health professionals deliver interventions that produce effective treatment outcomes.

Objective

This manual is primarily based on the principles of the Three-Part Model of Psychological Resilience (3-PR) model (de Terte et al., 2014), which suggested that factors such as cognition (optimism and adaptive coping), behaviours (adaptive health behaviours), and environment (social support, peer support) influence psychological resilience (de Terte et al., 2014).

Psychological resilience research incorporates the influences of internal and external constructs such as cognitions, behaviours, and environments in modifying levels of resilience in individuals (de Terte, 2017), thereby taking a personal adaptation mode of definition to a multidimensional one (de Terte, 2017; Pangallo et al., 2015). This manual supports the multidimensional definition of psychological resilience as an interactive concept contingent to various factors and not as a static trait of an individual, hence providing evidence that resilience can be built and is an ongoing process (Calitz & Santana, 2018; de Terte & Stephens, 2014; de Terte et al., 2009).

Psychological resilience is conceptualised as "the positive role of individual differences in people's response to stress and adversity" (Rutter, 1987, p. 316). Alternatively, coping consists of behavioural, cognitive, and environmental strategies used by resilient individuals to produce positive affect (Booth & Neill, 2017) to modify their behaviour and environment to reduce internal and external threats induced by stress or trauma (Gil, 2005; Weinberg et al., 2014) and to maintain well-being (Tugade & Fredrickson, 2004).

DOI: 10.4324/9781003256779-1

The PRTM is an innovative conception of an integrated psychological resilience treatment based on the 3-PR model, such as coping skills (passive and active coping), self-care behaviours, and social support (de Terte et al., 2014). It encompasses guided intervention modules, designed specifically to equip individuals with evidence-based strategies that rehabilitate personal potential to cope with daily stress, reduce stress, and increase general well-being without necessarily referencing a particular disorder, trauma, depression, or anxiety (Padesky & Mooney, 2012).

The PRTM aspires to be a "tool-box" (Muller, 2009) treatment intervention manual for health care professionals, who can utilise appropriate modules to either address specific areas for intervention or use the manual in its entirety to increase effective coping, reduce stress, and increase general well-being. The PRTM offers clients the opportunity to build their personal model of being resilient through life's adversities, to restore effective coping, and to provide a personal toolbox of skills.

Abstract and module overview

The PRTM is organised into four different guided intervention modules for therapists, with corresponding worksheets for clients. Each module encompasses four sessions, totalling 16 sessions. Worksheets are provided to the clients at the end of each session. Importantly, at the end of each module is the idea of relapse prevention.

The **passive coping module** describes strategies and the importance of acknowledging behaviours that distance individuals from stressors (i.e., venting, self-blame, self-distraction, denial, and behaviour disengagement) (Blow et al., 2017). This module introduces participants to the concept of recognising personal responsibilities in coping with stress, increasing personal utility, self-respect, individual autonomy, and planning effective initiatives. Participants will be also taught to identify and implement operative strategies to address avoidant behaviours, self-distraction, and denial in order to increase coping and reduce stress. Metacognitive activities (Nassif & Wells, 2014) will also be included as supplementary exercises to aid stress reduction and increase coping and general well-being.

The **self-care behaviour module** emphasises sets of behavioural activities that reduce the occurrence of both mental and physical health burdens (de Terte et al., 2014; LaVela et al., 2016). Self-care behaviours are self-determined activities (LaVela et al., 2016) carried out by individuals—such as physical exercises, practising self-compassion, and mindfulness activities (de Terte et al., 2014; Creswell et al., 2016)—that help improve both their mental and physical well-being. Clients will be invited to discuss their daily physical and dietary routine, the benefits of improving their activities, and obstacles that prevent them in attempting these suggested activities. These individuals will be taught ways to cope with daily stress by increasing personal awareness of thoughts and somatic feelings via practising mindfulness exercise. Practices such as self-compassion by acknowledging difficulties and being kind to the self, engaging in positive self-talk, and normalising failures and challenges are some of the strategies discussed in this module.

The **social support module** provides information to support clients in seeking social networks that offer psychological and material resources that benefit the individual's capacity to cope with stress (Cohen, 2004). In this module, the client's core understanding of social support will be explored. Clients will be encouraged to discuss their existing social support and other types of social support, such as information or cognitive, structural, emotional, material, and functional support (Sippel et al., 2015) that may or may not be accessible to them. Activities that will help clients identify barriers to accessing these types of support are included in this module.

The **active coping module** is based on the principles of CBT. This module encourages clients to challenge their irrational thoughts and behaviours for a desired outcome or consequence

(Roy et al., 2017). From a coping perspective, cognitive restructuring modifies the appraisal of an event or situation and allows for a reappraisal. Functional thoughts then replace maladaptive thoughts (Kohl et al., 2013). This module also provides clients with strategies for identifying their stress-related triggers, their cognitive reactions, and their present coping styles. Individual stress responses, such as succumbing, survival with impairment, resilience, and thriving (Steinhardt & Dolbier, 2008), are explored along with remedial adaptive coping strategies, such as problem-solving techniques, positive reframing, and using adaptive humour (Martin et al., 2003) to reduce daily stress. Grateful journaling, a supplementary exercise to enhance adaptive decision making, is also included.

Disclaimer

The PRTM is a treatment intervention manual designed to be delivered by registered psychologists, psychiatrists, and qualified CBT practitioners. Professionals are advised to deliver treatment in the order suggested by the manual to optimise outcomes.

The client population used in the development of this treatment manual consisted of adult individuals with subclinical stress presentations based on validated psychometric screenings. This was followed by a rigorous research assessment protocol, establishing a steady baseline for each client before any psychological interventions found in this treatment manual were administered.

With respect to the information available in this manual, neither the authors nor the publisher make any warranty or assume any legal liability or responsibility for patient referral appropriateness, accuracy, completeness, or clinical efficacy of the clinical interventions.

Professionals and organisations that utilise this manual and these modules are themselves *solely* responsible for the outcome of their clinical intervention with their respective patients or clients. In addition, any form of adaptation and replication of the information in this manual is strictly prohibited.

Recommendations to mental health professionals

Professionals are recommended to be cognisant and apply their clinical judgment and discretion at all times during sessions. General features and dimensions of effective psychiatric interview include these recommended techniques that encompass pivotal areas of verbal and nonverbal communication, listening and observation, behaviour, directiveness, and supportiveness (Silberman et al., 2015).

We recommend these techniques:

- Pause   **P**
- Listen   **L**
- Reflect   **R**
- Acknowledge   **A**
- Empathise appropriately   **E**
- Summarise   **S**

These techniques are pivotal in helping clinicians and mental health professionals assess client's perceptions, biases, and mental states. They will also allow for mental health professionals to reflect and provide a scouting period to arrive at a better understanding and evaluation of client's needs during sessions (Shea, 1998).

Bibliography

Blow, A. J., Bowles, R. P., Farero, A., Subramaniam, S., Lappan, S., Nichols, E., & Guty, D. (2017). Couples coping through deployment: Findings from a sample of national guard families. *Journal of Clinical Psychology, 73*(12), 1753–1767. https://doi.org/10.1002/jclp.22487

Booth, J. W., & Neill, J. T. (2017). Coping strategies and the development of psychological resilience. *Journal of Outdoor and Environmental Education, 20*(1), 47–54.

Calitz, C., & Santana, A. (2018). The art of health promotion: Linking research to practice. *American Journal of Health Promotion, 32*(3), 821–822. https://doi.org/10.1177/0890117118756180

Cohen, S. (2004). Social relationships and health. *American Psychologist, 9,* 676–684.

Creswell, J. D., Taren, A. A., Lindsay, E. K., Greco, C. M., Gianaros, P. J., Fairgrieve, A., . . . Ferris, J. L. (2016). Alterations in resting-state functional connectivity link mindfulness meditation with reduced interleukin-6: A randomized controlled trial. *Biological Psychiatry, 80*(1), 53–61. https://doi.org/10.1016/j.biopsych.2016.01.008

de Terte, I. (2017). The straw that broke the camel's back: A model psychological resilience to use with military personnel. In A. MacIntyre, D. Lagace-Roy, & D. R. Lindsay (Eds.), *Global views on military stress and resilience* (pp. 127–137). Winnipeg Publishing Office.

de Terte, I., Becker, J., & Stephens, C. (2009). An integrated model for understanding and developing resilience in the face of adverse events. *Journal of Pacific Rim Psychology, 3*(01), 20–26. https://doi.org/10.1375/prp.3.1.20

de Terte, I., Stephens, C., & Huddleston, L. (2014). The development of a three-part model of psychological resilience: Three part model of psychological resilience. *Stress and Health, 30*(5), 416–424. https://doi.org/10.1002/smi.2625

de Terte, I., & Stephens, C. (2014). Psychological resilience of workers in high-risk occupations: Guest editorial. *Stress and Health, 30*(5), 353–355. https://doi.org/10.1002/smi.2627

Gil, S. (2005). Coping style in predicting posttraumatic stress disorder among Israeli students. *Anxiety, Stress & Coping, 18*(4), 351–359. https://doi.org/10.1080/10615800500392732

Kohl, A., Rief, W., & Glombiewski, J. A. (2013). Acceptance, cognitive restructuring, and distraction as coping strategies for acute pain. *The Journal of Pain, 14*(3), 305–315. https://doi.org/10.1016/j.jpain.2012.12.005

LaVela, S. L., Etingen, B., & Miskevics, S. (2016). Factors influencing self-care behaviors in persons with spinal cord injuries and disorders. *Topics in Spinal Cord Injury Rehabilitation, 22*(1), 27–38. https://doi.org/10.1310/sci2201-27

Martin, R. A., Puhlik-Doris, P., Larsen, G., Gray, J., & Weir, K. (2003). Individual differences in uses of humor and their relation to psychological well-being: Development of the humor styles questionnaire. *Journal of Research in Personality, 37*(1), 48–75. https://doi.org/10.1016/S0092-6566(02)00534-2

Muller, R. (2009). The importance of resilience to primary care practitioners: An interactive psycho-social model. *Australasian Medical Journal, 1*(1), 1–15.

Nassif, Y., & Wells, A. (2014). Attention training reduces intrusive thoughts cued by a narrative of stressful life events: A controlled study: Attention training and intrusive thoughts. *Journal of Clinical Psychology, 70*(6), 510–517. https://doi.org/10.1002/jclp.22047

Padesky, C. A., & Mooney, K. A. (2012). Strengths-based cognitive-behavioural therapy: A four-step model to build resilience: Strengths-based CBT: Four steps to resilience. *Clinical Psychology & Psychotherapy, 19*(4), 283–290. https://doi.org/10.1002/cpp.1795

Pangallo, A., Zibarras, L., Lewis, R., & Flaxman, P. (2015). Resilience through the lens of interactionism: A systematic review. *Psychological Assessment, 27*(1), 1–20. https://doi.org/10.1037/pas0000024

Roy, R., Guha, R., Das Bhattacharya, S., & Mukhopadhyay, J. (2017). *Building a web based cognitive restructuring program for promoting resilience in a college campus* (pp. 520–524). IEEE. https://doi.org/10.1109/COMSNETS.2017.7945446

Rutter, M. (1987). Psychosocial resilience and protective mechanisms. *American Journal of Orthopsychiatry, 57*(3), 316–331.

Shea, S. C. (1998). *Psychiatric interviewing: The art of understanding: A practical guide for psychiatrists, psychologists, counselors, social workers, nurses, and other mental health professionals.* Saunders.

Silberman, E. K., Certa, K., & Kay, A. (2015). The psychiatric interview: Settings and techniques. In A. Tasman, J. Kay, J. A. Lieberman, M. B. First, & M. B. Riba (Eds.), *Psychiatry* (pp. 34–55). https://doi.org/10.1002/9781118753378.ch3

Sippel, L. M., Pietrzak, R. H., Charney, D. S., Mayes, L. C., & Southwick, S. M. (2015). How does social support enhance resilience in the trauma-exposed individual? *Ecology and Society, 20*(4). https://doi.org/10.5751/ES-07832-200410

Steinhardt, M., & Dolbier, C. (2008). Evaluation of a resilience intervention to enhance coping strategies and protective factors and decrease symptomatology. *Journal of American College Health, 56*(4), 445–453. https://doi.org/10.3200/JACH.56.44.445-454

Tugade, M. M., & Fredrickson, B. L. (2004). Resilient individuals use positive emotions to bounce back from negative emotional experiences. *Journal of Personality and Social Psychology, 86*(2), 320–333. https://doi.org/10.1037/0022-3514.86.2.320

Weinberg, M., Gil, S., & Gilbar, O. (2014). Forgiveness, coping, and terrorism: Do tendency to forgive and coping strategies associate with the level of posttraumatic symptoms of injured victims of terror attacks?: Forgiveness, coping strategies, and terrorism. *Journal of Clinical Psychology, 70*(7), 693–703. https://doi.org/10.1002/jclp.22056

MODULE 1

PASSIVE COPING

Overview

The purpose of this four-session module is to identify passive coping strategies. The identification of passive coping strategies will reduce stress, achieve effective coping, and increase psychological resilience (Deasy et al., 2014; Mayordomo et al., 2016).

Goals

The goal is to help client's explore current passive coping strategies used to mitigate stress. This module explores strategies and advantages to increase general well-being and reduce stress. Supplementary exercises such as metacognitive activities, which contribute to a decrease in stress, are also included. Clients will work towards developing a personalised plan to reduce stress.

Materials needed

- Module 1: Passive coping
- Client worksheets: Passive coping

Module overview

The passive coping module introduces clients to sets of cognitive and behavioural strategies that will help them regulate stress responses, cope effectively, reduce stress levels, and increase general well-being.

Session 1: The psychology of coping and venting

- Sustaining and strengthening therapeutic relationship with client
- Fundamentals of coping
  - Modified operational model of stress and coping

DOI: 10.4324/9781003256779-2

- Passive coping—exploring venting behaviour
  • Role-play technique

In the first session, the therapist explores the client's ability to cope with challenges during stressful situations. Clients are encouraged to consider the benefits and disadvantages of using a passive coping strategy (i.e., venting) both in a short or extended period. Clients are then challenged to apply both cognitive and behavioural strategies to make venting an adaptive coping process.

Session 2: Reviewing behaviour disengagement and self-distraction activities

— Passive coping—discussing behaviour disengagement and self-distraction as coping strategies

In the second session, the therapist discusses two other types of passive coping: behaviour disengagement and self-distraction activities. Behaviour disengagement tendencies and self-distraction activities are reviewed with clients on their effectiveness in increasing adaptive coping efforts and retaining clients' goals. Cognitive appraisal and behavioural strategies such as planning are then applied to increase adaptive coping to reduce stress and increase well-being.

Session 3: Addressing self-blame and denial tendencies

— Passive coping—self-blame and denial tendencies
  • Role-play technique

In the third session, the therapist explores self-blame and denial tendencies. Benefits and disadvantages of both self-blame and denial tendencies are discussed. Clients are then taught cognitive and behavioural techniques, with a focus on compassion techniques to reduce self-blame. This is followed by a role-playing exercise that will help clients observe self-blame statements and understand the benefits of applying compassion-focused cognitive and behavioural strategies in increasing adaptive coping. Denial as a coping strategy is also discussed. Both the importance and drawbacks of using this coping technique are explored. Contributing factors such as attention, thoughts, avoidant behaviour, and language are reviewed with the client to increase adaptive coping behaviour. The concept of acceptance and relevant exercises are then introduced to reduce denial tendencies.

Session 4: Metacognition and relapse prevention exercises

  • Inquiring how they have been using coping strategies in past weeks
  • Metacognitive activities

In the final session, clients are taught supplementary exercises, such as metacognitive exercises, to increase adaptive decision making. In addition, relapse prevention exercises are incorporated in this session to increase client adherence to learning.

Appendix A

Client worksheets for passive coping module

Session 1: Introduction

Therapist to client:

- Welcomes and thanks client for attending the session
- Reassures client that their issues matter
- Reassures and normalise that emotional distress is not a sign of weakness
- It is unique to everyone

T: In this module, ways of how one can cope best with daily challenges and during difficult times are discussed. Perhaps the questions to begin with are "What are your personal views of coping?" and "How do you generally cope with challenges?"

Note to therapist:

It is recommended that therapist take notes intermittently during sessions as a way to:

- Accurately retain information on client's thoughts, feelings, and behaviours
- Help during reflection sessions
- Indicate progress that has been made

Therapist can gently probe client's understanding of the term "coping."

T: According to research, coping plays an important role in the way an individual deals with their day-to-day challenges (Mayordomo et al., 2016) and is fundamental to one's social functioning (Carver & Connor-Smith, 2010).

Coping strategies are also identified as "conscious, intentional, and mostly adaptive" (Cramer, 2008) ways to cope during stress. Research in coping has evolved from viewing coping as a style or trait to more of a process that changes over time in relation to the situation (Lazarus, 1993). Hence, coping is not static but modifiable.

Note to therapist:

Therapist is encouraged to explain the diagram modified operational model of stress and coping (Goh et al., 2010) (see Figure 1.1) and use it to identify general or specific examples on how clients normally cope.

Therapist will also need to briefly explain the definitions of cognitive appraisal, active and passive coping, adaptive behaviour, and psychological resilience.

Cognitive appraisal explains a process when an individual assesses if an event is vital to their well-being through utilising both primary and secondary cognitive appraisals.

In primary appraisal, the individual evaluates the risks or benefits to their self-esteem or if the well-being of loved ones is at stake. Values, belief about self and the world, goals, and commitments are activated to evaluate the situation perceived as stressful.

The secondary appraisal allows the individual to decide ways to overcome, reduce, or prevent harm or improve the situation (Booth & Neill, 2017; Crane et al., 2018).

The primary appraisal of a perceived threat leads in turn to the secondary appraisal, which activates a coping response to manage the situation (Folkman et al., 1986).

Active coping: Active coping refers to purposeful ways to deal with problems and seek comfort and social support (Barendregt et al., 2015).

Passive coping strategies are defined as inactive tactics employed to avoid disagreements and conflicts among people or institutions (Li, 2014). Passive coping strategies include behaviours such as denial, mental disengagement, and behavioural disengagement (Blow et al., 2017).

Adaptive behaviour: Adaptive behaviours are coping strategies utilised during difficult times to maintain well-being (Tugade & Fredrickson, 2004) and are effective psychological constructs in building psychological resilience in individuals (de Terte et al., 2014).

Psychological resilience: Psychological resilience interventions have the potential to be an inoculation effort, teaching individuals to adapt to their daily stressors (Meichenbaum, 1988). Psychological resilience is an interactive concept, contingent to various factors and not a static trait of an individual. Hence, it provides evidence that resilience can be learnt and is an ongoing process (Calitz & Santana, 2018; de Terte et al., 2014).

Psychological resilience incorporates robust, resilient, multidimensional building constructs such as coping skills, self-efficacy, self-care, social support, and acceptance (de Terte et al., 2014; Hayes, 2004). Psychological resilience also has the potential to act as a protective factor that contributes to resilience building and effective coping (Enns et al., 2016; Booth & Neill, 2017).

HOW DO I COPE?

STRESS/THREAT

Cognitive appraisal

Primary appraisal (process of perceiving a threat to oneself)

Secondary appraisal (process of recalling a potential response to the threat)

COPING
process of executing that response

Active Coping

Passive Coping

Behaviour

Adaptive Behaviour

Nonadaptive Behaviour

OUTCOME

Increased Psychological Resilience

Decreased Psychological Resilience

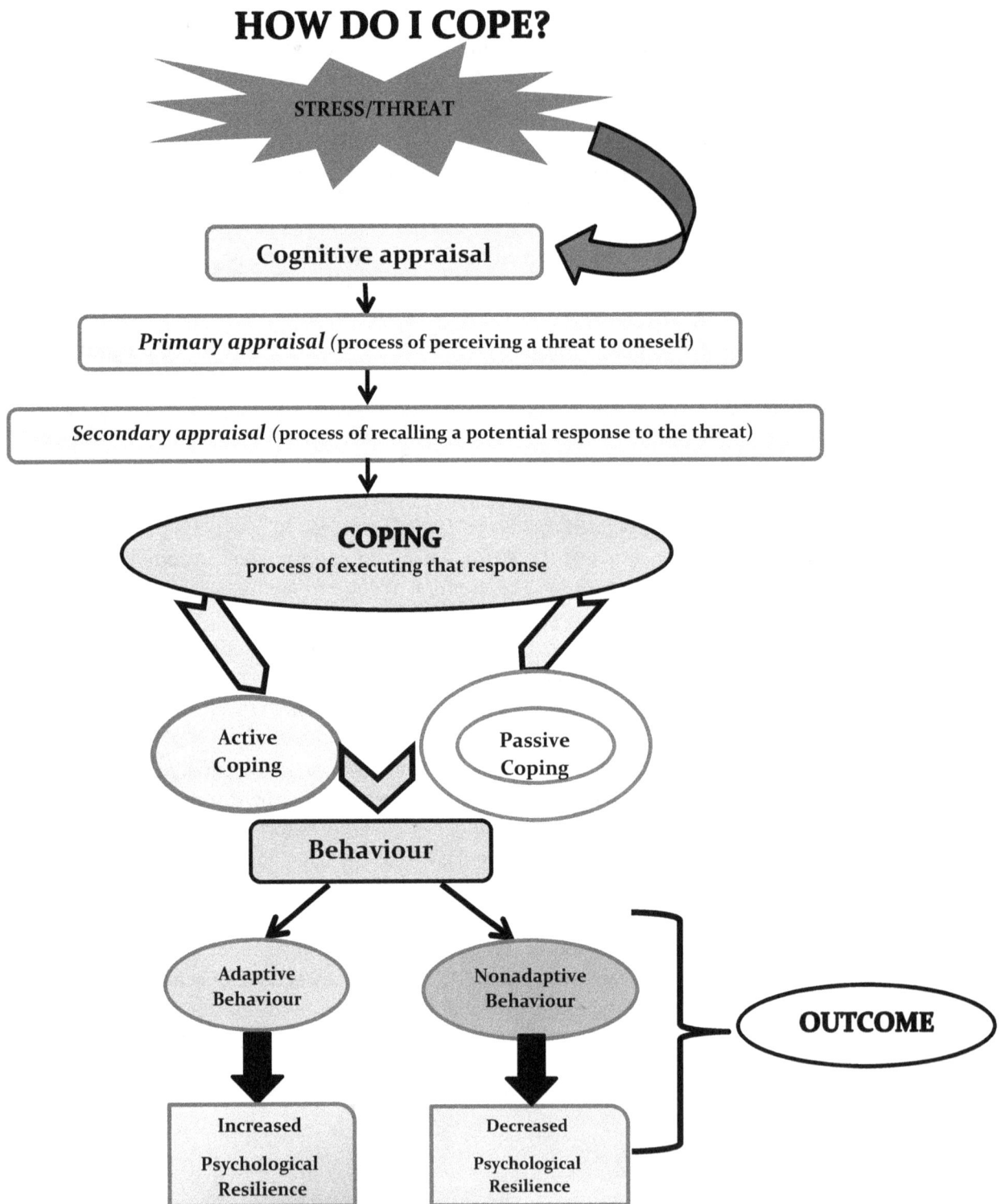

Figure 1.1 Modified operational model of stress and coping (passive coping)

Note: *Adapted from "The Revised Transactional Model (RTM) of Occupational Stress and Coping: An Improved Process Approach," by Goh, Sawang, & Oei, 2010.* The Australian and New Zealand Journal of Organisational Psychology, 3, *13–20. Copyright 2010 by Yong Goh.*

T: This diagram explains how an individual generally copes.

T: Now for a closer look at passive coping. In this module, the focus will be how one can identify and effectively manage passive coping strategies to reduce stress and increase well-being.

T: Perhaps begin by exploring your personal understanding about the term "venting".

Note to therapist: Note the initial understanding of the term "venting" for client.

T: Venting is an emotional expression of anger—either verbal, physical, or written—where individuals often remain angry after the venting interaction but feel better (Parlamis, 2012).

T: Perhaps recall a stressful event that required venting (i.e., stress event)?

T: What was the reason for choosing venting as a coping strategy (i.e., cognitive appraisal)?

T: Whom was the venting directed to?

T: What was your behaviour like around the person or situation that caused the venting?

T: In your opinion, was venting useful?

Note to therapist: Explore if venting allowed client to have temporary relief.

T: Has there been a time when you did not feel much relief after venting?

T: What is your opinion on what was different?

T: Was there perhaps something related to the response(s) received?

Note to therapist: Probe further into the differences in the responses that client received from the person they were venting to. Research says that venting positively impacts their general mood or overall affect; individuals often remain angry after the venting interaction but feel better.

T: Now is a good time to begin a role play about venting. Do your best in reenacting the venting conversation.

Note to therapist: Take note of the "blaming language" that may be used in role play, as this may contribute to greater postventing anger. Addressing it appropriately will largely change the consequences or stress response.

Therapist notes:

T: From the role play, "blaming language" was observed to express the event with that individual. Some of the examples of blaming language observed were:

T: Blaming language is the acknowledgement of responsibility used during venting.
T: There are some importance differences between venting and blaming language.

While venting is an emotional expression of anger—either verbal, physical, or written—where individuals often remain angry after the venting interaction but feel better, blaming language is the acknowledgement of responsibility used during venting.

It is important to reframe statements used in the venting process that may increase self-awareness that one is engaging in an incorrect form of coping. This may increase personal accountability in reducing stress (Parlamis, 2012).

T: What are your thoughts about that?
T: Now we can learn how to reduce "blaming language" so one does not remain angry and cope poorly.
T: It is fine to vent to reduce acute frustration; however, if one continues to ruminate and vent, this may lead to nonadaptive behaviour, which consequently results in poor coping, reduced psychological resilience and well-being, and increased stress symptoms.
T: Perhaps during this week, practise:
- Taking note of the "blame language" that was used to describe an event that may instigate negative emotions and monitor your mood by using a mood graph
T: A mood graph is a simple yet effective way to assist individuals in recognising their mood states. In this way, one can directly link mood to behaviour change or behaviour reinforcement (Saunders et al., 2017).
T: Explain daily mood graph to client.

> **Note to therapist:** The mood graph allows individuals to track their mood states at regular intervals. This exercise of charting mood states helps identify patterns in individuals for how their mood differs over times and circumstances.

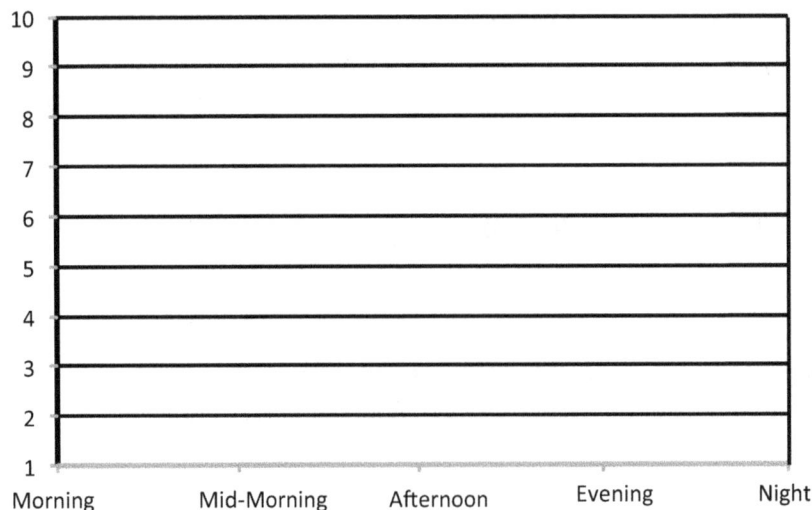

Figure 1.2 Mood tracking graph

Description:

1: Low Mood
10: Elated

- It is okay to feel uncomfortable when trying new approaches
- When "something doesn't work," look at what "something" means
    a. What were your attempts to change the circumstances?
    b. Were the expectations too much or too fast?

T: In the next session, both behaviour disengagements and self-distraction that are sometimes present as obstacles in reducing stress, and ways to choose effective coping strategies, will be discussed.

Note to therapist:

- Ask if client needs further clarification about the session
- Encourage client to attempt assignment for this session in Appendix A: Session 1

Ψ Collaborative tasks checklist

- Explored client's ability to cope with challenges during stressful situations
- Introduced client to the fundamentals of coping
- Discussed passive coping strategies (i.e., venting), and benefits and disadvantages of using this strategy both in a short or extended period
- Guided client in being able to apply both cognitive and behavioural strategies to make venting an adaptive coping process

Session 2: Introduction

Therapist asks how the client has been generally feeling in the last week.

- Welcomes client back into the second session in the passive coping module
- Discusses how their week was

T: In today's session, perhaps the question to begin with is "What makes one want to reduce efforts or give up on personal goals?"

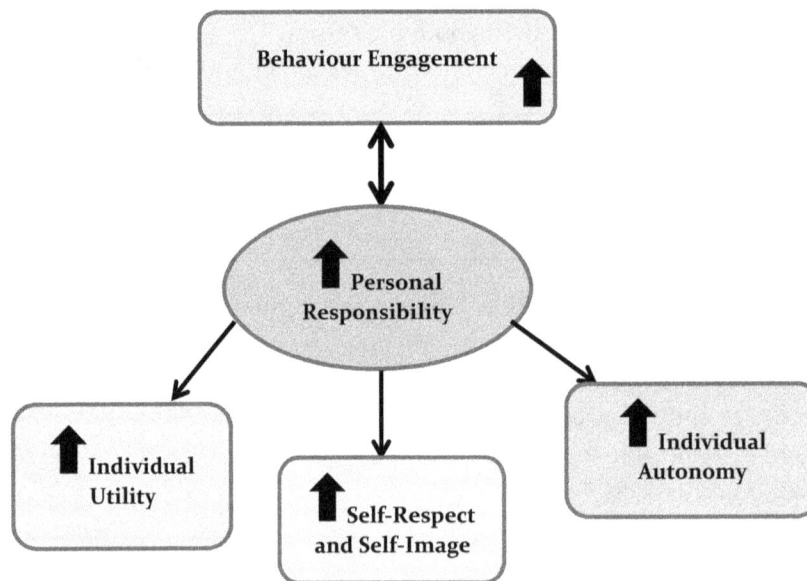

Figure 1.3 Schematic diagram of personal responsibility and behavioural disengagement in innocent bystanders during classroom management events

Note: *Adapted from "Personal responsibility and behavioral disengagement in innocent bystanders during classroom management events: The moderating effect of teacher aggressive tendencies," by Montuoro & Lewis, 2018. The Journal of Educational Research, 111(4), p. 439–445. Copyright 2018 by Ramon Lewis.*

T: Explain these definitions to client:

Behaviour disengagement is quitting or withdrawing effort from the attempt to attain the goal. **Self-distraction** often occurs when conditions prevent behaviour disengagement. Self-distraction activities serve to distract an individual or act as an escape strategy. Examples may include daydreaming, excessive sleeping, watching television, and presumably current distractions such as internet surfing, streaming, and indulging in social media.

Behaviour Disengagement

T: What are your thoughts or experiences regarding withdrawing effort from a goal or an attempt? It could be a recent event or something that happened in the past.
T: Perhaps elaborate on how it was handled?
T: What types of behavioural disengagement activities caused the withdrawal of effort from your personal goals?

T: What were the outcomes?

T: Did they provide continuous relief?

T: Perhaps explain about other times when behavioural disengagement activities were successfully avoided

T: What are some examples?

Therapist notes:

T: What are some of your personal goals?

- Were the goals too difficult?
- Were the expectations for a successful outcome too low or too high?
- Were there any stress cues that required your disengagement from goals that were perceived as unattainable?

Note to therapist: Explore client's previous experience of behaviour disengagement.

Therapist notes:

T: In retrospective, what are the things that could have been done differently?

Scientific research (Montuoro et al., 2018) has shown that one way of looking at reducing the tendency of giving up on our goals, also called "behaviour disengagement," is by increasing personal responsibility. This does not imply that we are irresponsible people but that planning and being conscious about our goals allows for better outcomes.

(Examples of personal responsibility include activities that you take to gain and maintain paid employment, following through with academic pursuits, friendships, and relationships, and these have utility-enhancing consequences that are intrinsically satisfying.)

T: Do you have any current goals?

T: Does achieving a current goal allow for gains in further opportunities, such as scholarships, employment, work promotion, better salary, good relationship, or a healthier body?

> **Note to therapist**: Observe the client's body language, which may depict excitement, regret, or disappointment regarding their future goal.

T: How does the thought of achieving your goal feel?
- Scientific research (Montuoro et al., 2018) also has shown that pursuing a goal may foster self-respect, which is defined as the positive impression of oneself and personal autonomy (examples of fostering self-respect include activities that increase positive feeling or sense or lead to feelings of mastery and enhanced self-image), and that activities that increase personal autonomy occur when individuals are vigilant about making good choices and effective long-term planning

T: How impactful are your choices on the outcome of the goal?

T: Are there any obstacles that are in the way of achieving these goals?

T: Are the goals still worth pursuing? Why?

> **Note to therapist**: Summarise information from client to this point.

> **Therapist notes:**

T: Based on today's session, your personal goals are ones that are able to:

> **Note to therapist**: Reflect on client's answers to select the boxes. Feel free to add accordingly.

- Increase your individual utility (e.g., such as gaining and maintaining paid employment and have utility-enhancing consequences that are intrinsically satisfying)
- Enhance your self-respect and self-image (e.g., positive feeling, sense, or leading to feelings of mastery and enhanced self-image)
- Foster personal autonomy (e.g., making good choices and effective long-term planning)
- Other

Table 1.1 Tracking personal responsibilities and goal achievements

Increase your individual utility

Enhance your self-respect and self-image

Foster personal autonomy

T: Perhaps this is a good time to explore ways of reducing obstacles and increasing opportunities to positively influence these areas in your life (i.e., increased behaviour engagement and successful outcomes).

T: Perhaps explain some obstacles that could be hindering your coping or progress.

T: Are there any concerns about how positive opportunities may change things that are now familiar?

T: What are your personal aspirations?

T: Are there any worries or reservations about these aspirations?

T: Are there concerns about how your thoughts and behaviour can sometimes stand in the way of achieving future goals?

T: What are the opportunities that are available to enhance all three of these areas (i.e., increase individual utility, enhance self-respect and self-image, and fostering personal autonomy)?

T: Do these opportunities potentially enhance work, personal, and familial well-being or academic opportunities?

T: What are some of your influences or strategies that can help contribute to those opportunities?

T: Do these strategies assist in improving views of self and personal self-respect?

T: Here are some action strategies that can further decrease behaviour disengagement and self-distractions:
- Time management
- Skills enhancement
- Reducing distracting activities and behaviours
- Adjusting expectations

Note to therapist: Encourage client to be vigilant about red flags for behaviour disengagement by exploring difficulty levels and expectations of achieving their current and future goals.

Red flags for behaviour disengagement

Table 1.2 Red flags for behaviour disengagement

Initial warning signs or stress cues	Difficulties in achieving goals (0-10) 0 = No difficulty 10 = Extreme difficulty	Expectations for success (0-10) 0 = Low success 10 = High success

T: Now to explore other ways in which one copes. These coping techniques can be beneficial and equally distract individuals from achieving their goals and achieving well-being.

Note to therapist: RECAP: Self-distraction often occurs when conditions prevent behavioural disengagement. It serves to distract individuals or acts as an escape strategy from the goal with which the stressor is interfering.

T: Is this familiar? Perhaps you can think of some examples?
T: How did these activities influence outcomes (i.e., stress levels)?
T: Are some activities still used? Are they useful or not?

Note to therapist: Summarise information from client to this point. Acknowledge that while distractions can be a healthy coping technique, it is equally important not to allow these distractions to hinder progress or create setbacks.

Handling setbacks

Handling setbacks or anticipating circumstances that may incite a relapse is important for maintaining progress. Being vigilant of high-risk situations, thoughts, and actions that could interact in the development and maintenance of problems is one way to help sustain positive outcomes (Thakker & Ward, 2010).

Table 1.3 Managing and tracking behaviours that lead to setback

What led to the relapse?	My thoughts	My behaviour	What I would do differently

T: In the next session, the use of self-blame and denial to cope through difficult times will be discussed.

Note to therapist:

- Ask if client needs any further clarification
- Encourage client to attempt assignment for this session in Appendix A: Session 2

Ψ Collaborative tasks checklist

- Explained two other variants of passive coping
  - Behaviour disengagement (i.e., individual utility, self-respect and self-image, and personal autonomy)
    - Self-distraction activities
- Behaviour disengagement tendencies and self-distraction activities were reviewed with client on their effectiveness in increasing adaptive coping efforts and retaining client's goals
- Cognitive appraisal and behavioural strategies such as planning (i.e., time management) were explored to increase adaptive coping

Session 3: Introduction

Therapist to client:
Therapist asks how the client has been generally feeling in the last week.

- Welcomes client back into the third session in the passive coping module
- Discusses how their week was

T: In today's session, the use of self-blame and denial to cope during challenging times will be discussed.

T: Self-blame is a form of passive coping that happens when one excessively criticises and blames oneself.

T: Are these types of thoughts and behaviours familiar? Have you used them in the past, or even currently?

T: Perhaps relate an experience that caused these thoughts and behaviours of self-blame.

Note to therapist: Therapist is recommended to explore if there has been history of anxiety, depression, emotional abuse, poor self-worth, unresolved guilt, failures, or childhood or recent trauma experience. Feelings of disgust and anger are also common among individuals who have experienced the above.

(McLean et al., 2018)

T: How much of doing that was a relief?

T: Has self-blame been a useful coping mechanism?

T: Perhaps elaborate on your stress and well-being levels when indulged in self-blame.

T: Are there any fears of letting go of self-blame?

Note to therapist: Therapist is encouraged to probe when self-blame as a coping strategy has worked for the client. Explore the source; was it in their past, during a specific phase (i.e., childhood)? Do not force an answer; respect client's choice not to discuss further.

Note to therapist: Therapist can further explain that self-blame acts as an ongoing internal threat to a person's sense of identity and self-perception (Ehlers & Clark, 2000). This allows continuous negative appraisal to maintain the views of personal incompetence and inability to cope that worsen self-blame.

T: What is the alternative? How would it feel not to be critical of yourself?

T: Scientific research (Neff, 2016) indicates that cognitive and behavioural strategies with focus on compassion techniques help reduce self-blame.

T: Now for some activities.

Here are some objects (i.e., a tennis ball, a lemon, or an orange). Alternatively, a personal object is fine to use; it could be a scarf or a sock that can held, worn, or touched when one feels judged or criticised or starts to self-blame. This sensory technique acts as a reminder to start an internal compassion-focused conversation, which allows for better control over how one perceives stress or a threat.

T: Now for a role-play session.

Choose any one of these objects and use them as soothing objects. Then, think about a common self-blame statement that is often used, and then focus on the object. Think about how the object feels in your hand or how it smells. Accompany this act with a compassionate statement, such as "I feel this way because I do this to protect myself, and that does not make me feel bad or weak."

Note to therapist: Therapist is recommended to note both the self-blame and statements client uses and to encourage client to discuss more examples if required.

T: Good try!

T: What was your experience in using this technique?

T: Was this compassion-focused activity helpful in providing some relief during stressful situations, thoughts, or circumstances?

Note to therapist: Here, therapist can further probe on the difference that client observed when applying this soothing and grounding exercise (Gilbert & Procter, 2006).

T: Perhaps it would be useful to note ways that one can appraise, think about, and react (behave) to stressful situations while applying this technique.

T: What are your thoughts about being more able to achieve and pursue your goals for the week without self-blame tendencies getting in your way?

T: It may be a good idea to practise this exercise over the coming week, and perhaps keep a journal of the compassionate statements that are used. Remember that these statements are your own.

T: Another form of passive coping that will be discussed in this session is denial. Scientific evidence has indicated that individuals often use denial as a coping technique when requiring more time to digest and monitor a threat before using a more adaptive coping style. Denial is viewed as functional in the early stage of coping (Miceli & Castelfranchi, 1998).

T: What are your experiences in using this technique to cope with challenges?

T: What are some of causal factors or events that triggered the use of denial?

T: How did that work out at the beginning?

T: Have there been any disadvantages?

Note to therapist: A requirement for denial is that an individual is aware of the information that they have received (Wheeler & Lord, 1999). However, the individual interprets it according to their reality. Denial is also known as a mechanism to protect the individual's ego from excessive stress (Miceli & Castelfranchi, 1998). Researchers have noted that denial is triggered by anxious thoughts about losing self-esteem, control, assistance, or protection (Aspinwall & Brunhart, 1996) or by perceived threats to the individual (Wheeler & Lord, 1999).

Note to therapist: Therapist can discuss challenging outcomes due to denial, such as isolation, delay in seeking appropriate health care, interference with the rights of others, and psychosomatic disorders.

Here, therapist needs to carefully and consciously apply active listening, being aware of changes in the discrepancies between client's behaviour and conversation while offering them a safe environment in which to acquire more adaptive coping techniques (Wheeler & Lord, 1999). This is best done before recommendations and therapeutic exercises are provided to clients.

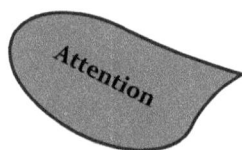

Attention

T: Now to look at some adaptive ways to move forward. This can be done by observing how attention to self and others, thoughts, behaviours, and language are utilised to reduce denial and increase acceptance (Corio et al., 2017; Freire et al., 2018; Gloria & Steinhardt, 2016).

T: Now to explore the first component: attention, and more specifically, how one pays attention to self and others. Often, attention goes both inwards (self-focus), monitoring how an individual feels that they come across to others, and outwards (others-focus), paying attention to how others behave around the individual.

Thoughts

T: Later in this session, we will explore strategies to allow attention-provoking behaviours and thoughts to pass, without needing them to be different or for circumstances to change.

T: Now to explore the second component: thoughts. During stressful situations, individuals often worry about a situation before it happens (anticipatory worry), while it is happening (mind-reading), and after the situation (post-analysis). Again, observing these thoughts and distancing self from them would encourage acceptance.

Note to therapist: Here, therapist briefly defines terminologies such as anticipatory worry, mind-reading, and post-analysis.

Anticipatory worry: Worrying about the future outcomes.

Mind-reading: An act of assuming what others think about you.

Post-analysis: Ruminations or excessive evaluation of the circumstances that have happened in the past.

Avoidant Behaviour

T: During stressful times and events, it is quite common for individuals to prevent stressful situations by applying denial to keep safe or to avoid the situation at all costs.

Denial leads to avoidance (Wheeler & Lord, 1999). Avoidance is often a first reaction that people have in response to anxious situations. At times, individuals attempt to avoid an anxiety-provoking situation by taking steps to alter form and frequency of avoidant behaviour, which may cause further behavioural harm. The drawback is that by avoiding such situations, reentering similar situations becomes more difficult and, inevitably, delay or sabotage an individual's value and goal pursuits.

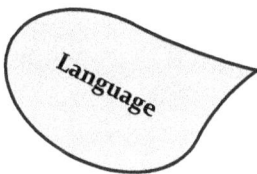

Language

T: The tendency to phrase anxious emotions and thoughts into everyday language is quite common. Some examples include:

"I feel anxious when I drive" or "I will surely feel anxious during my exams". Using specific words such as "paperwork", "internal investigation", and "work performance review" may trigger or call to mind anxious feelings. Hence, avoiding anxiety-triggering situations alone may not be beneficial to reduce anxiety.

T: Now to explore some cognitive behavioural strategies for reversing nonadaptive attention, thoughts, behaviours, and language to reduce denial and increase acceptance.

Table 1.4 Attention: Self-focus and others-focus

Attention
Self-Focus
Others-Focus

The alternative is to pay attention to these thoughts and feelings, and allow the self to experience the situation as it is and not to be nonjudgemental.

Table 1.5 Tracking anticipatory worry, mind-reading, and post-analysis thoughts

Thoughts
Anticipatory worry
Mind-reading
Post-analysis

The alternative is to distance oneself or use imagery techniques where anxiety-provoking thoughts are replaced by more soothing images or grateful thoughts (i.e., leaves flowing down a stream or thanking the mind for all types of thoughts and not reacting impulsively) (Stahl & Goldstein, 2010).

Avoidant behaviours

1

2

3

4

The alternative is to prioritise the benefits of achieving these values and goals and remind yourself of them during anxiety-provoking activities.

Language:

1

2

3

4

The alternative is to recognise trigger words that increase anxiety and be conscious of the usage and meaning of these words in self-talk and conversations.

Therapist notes:

T: Now to explore how acceptance is defined.

Acceptance is an individual's willingness to embrace, rather than tolerate negative or stressful internal experiences during a difficult experience (Charbonneau, 2017; Hayes, 2004). Acceptance is noted to facilitate decentring—a cognitive action that allows an individual to view stressful thoughts and feelings as unavoidable and temporary (Charbonneau, 2017). Acceptance is also characterized as a "special kind of positive thinking consisting in reframing or 'redirecting' frustration itself, by finding in it some opportunity for goal pursuit and satisfaction" (Miceli & Castelfranchi, 2001, p. 116).

T: Perhaps discuss times in your life when acceptance has been utilised to reduce stress.

T: In your opinion, was it useful?

T: Are you willing to apply or utilise acceptance to reduce stress?

Therapist notes:

T: Earlier in the session, the concept of acceptance was discussed. Now we will explore the concept of willingness. Willingness is a marker of acceptance and enhances engagement during stressful tasks. Increase in willingness was associated with reduced distress, improved functioning in individuals, and reduced avoidance (Reid et al., 2017). Practising and applying willingness encourages individuals to deal with difficult obsessions or anxiety without trying to prevent or alter these inner experiences (Reid et al., 2017).

T: Scientific research has shown that individuals who were more willing to accept negative thoughts were able to focus attention towards a goal instead of suppressing negative thoughts (Reid et al., 2017).

T: What is your personal definition of willingness?

Therapist notes:

T: Perhaps recount a stressful situation to which willingness can be applied to reduce stress and pursue values and goals.

Remember that willingness is not to give in but to embrace unwanted stress or anxiety without trying to inhibit or change these inner experiences.

T: Perhaps those who are more willing to experience their worries, fears, and anxieties may have more focus to allocate toward task goals because less effort is spent suppressing thoughts or emotional experiences.

Note to therapist:

- Explore how the client has understood the terms "acceptance" and "willingness" in the past

---

T: Using the same goal or another goal, how would one use willingness to increase attention where it matters most?

T: Another benefit that comes from cultivating willingness is that one may be able to embrace less stressful events with greater ease and thus have new and positive experiences.

Note to therapist:

- Ask if client needs further clarification
- Encourage client to attempt assignment for this session in Appendix A: Session 3

Ψ Collaborative tasks checklist

- Therapist has introduced and explained to client both self-blame and denial tendencies, their benefits and drawbacks
- Compassion techniques and compassion-focused cognitive and behavioural strategies have been explored with client in increasing personal adaptive coping
- Contributing factors such as attention, thoughts, avoidant behaviour, and language have been reviewed with client to increase adaptive coping
- The concepts of acceptance and willingness have been introduced to reduce denial tendencies

Session 4: Introduction

Therapist to client
Therapist asks how the client has been generally feeling in the last week.

- Welcomes client back into the fourth session in the passive coping module
- Discusses how their week was

T: Today is the fourth and final session in the passive coping module. This session will explore metacognitive strategies and relapse prevention exercises.

T: A form of metacognitive strategy known as metacognitive monitoring exercise is a supplementary coping technique. This metacognitive monitoring exercise helps in reducing intrusive thoughts and stimulating adaptive action.

According to the metacognitive model of stress-related intrusions by Nassif et al. (2014), metacognition awareness through auditory stimuli reduces intrusive thoughts to "background noise" or interruptions and reduces poor coping.

The PRTM uses a simple number countdown of 10, 9, 8, 7, 6, 5, 4, 3, 2, 1 (from 10), and say "CHANGE" or any other effective metacognitive exercises to reduce intrusive thoughts and stimulate adaptive actions.

T: Perhaps when a negative thought pops into one's mind that either makes one evaluate negatively or causes a sense of wrongness or uncertainty that may sound like "I am not good enough", "I can't do this", "I am not prepared for the exam", "I can't deal with that transfer or deployment", "I am not well", or "I am lonely", then apply a method such as counting down from 10, 9, 8, 7, 6, 5, 4, 3, 2, 1 and say "**CHANGE**" or "**RESET**" and choose an Adaptive action. Feel free to use positive phrases, poems, or songs to stimulate adaptive actions.

Example:

1. Think about a moderately stressful situation or thought that has been on your mind during the last week
2. Now, stand up and stretch a little
3. Say "10, 9, 8, 7, 6, 5, 4, 3, 2, 1" and "Change"
4. Then quickly write down **an adaptive action** specific to that intrusive thought (i.e., stop fiddling with the phone, read the first line of the journal article, write a positive statement, get out of bed, get to the gym, or call a friend)
5. **Reflect:** With a plan of action in your hands, choose either to:
   - **Apply** (i.e., activities that bring improvement or resolution to the problem); or
   - **Avoid** (i.e., activities which might delay the discomfort for a while but maintain the problem)

T: Thoughts that are both functional and dysfunctional are directly linked to how one behaves. Metacognitive exercises such as this one can be used to regain a sense of control and functional thought patterns to reduce anxiety and worry.

T: What is your opinion about this strategy being useful in reducing stressful thoughts?

T: As for relapse prevention planning, this exercise is not just about encouraging one to attempt the worksheets that are made available but instead simply to get back on track as soon as possible.

- Give yourself time and do not try to force it
- Make regular practice of your goals and avoid judging your efforts too strenuously

These exercises are not meant to judge or to be a competition. They are meant to be informative and enable one to discover individual coping levels and increase personal resilience in order to reduce stress. It is important to be cognisant, aware, or foresee any problems in carrying out tasks and to address them promptly.

My setback prevention plan (relative to topics discussed in Module 1)

I My self-talk

1

2

3

4

5

II How I choose to cope

1

2

3

III How will my life change if I have a setback?

1

2

3

IV My action plans

1

2

3

Note to therapist:

- Ask if client needs further clarification
- Encourage clients to attempt assignment for this session in Appendix A: Session 4

Ψ Collaborative tasks checklist

- Supplementary exercises, such as a metacognition exercise, have been introduced
- Relapse prevention exercises have been explained and understood by client

---

Bibliography

Aspinwall, L. G., & Brunhart, S. M. (1996). Distinguishing optimism from Denial: Optimistic beliefs predict attention to health threats. *Personality and Social Psychology Bulletin, 22*(10), 993–1003.

Barendregt, C. S., Van der Laan, A. M., Bongers, I. L., & Van Nieuwenhuizen, C. (2015). Adolescents in secure residential care: The role of active and passive coping on general well-being and self-esteem. *European Child & Adolescent Psychiatry, 24*(7), 845–854. https://doi.org/10.1007/s00787-014-0629-5

Blow, A. J., Bowles, R. P., Farero, A., Subramaniam, S., Lappan, S., Nichols, E., & Guty, D. (2017). Couples coping through deployment: Findings from a sample of national guard families. *Journal of Clinical Psychology, 73*(12), 1753–1767. https://doi.org/10.1002/jclp.22487

Booth, J. W., & Neill, J. T. (2017). Coping strategies and the development of psychological resilience. *Journal of Outdoor and Environmental Education, 20*(1), 47–54.

Calitz, C., & Santana, A. (2018). The art of health promotion: Linking research to practice. *American Journal of Health Promotion, 32*(3), 821–822. https://doi.org/10.1177/0890117118756180

Carver, C. S., & Connor-Smith, J. (2010). Personality and coping. *Annual Review of Psychology, 61*, 679–704. doi: 10.1146/annurev.psych.093008.100352

Charbonneau, D. (2017). Mindfulness and acceptance: How do they relate to stress and resilience? In A. MacIntyre, D. Lagace-Roy, & D. R. Lindsay (Eds.), *Global views on military stress and resilience* (pp. 239–256). Winnipeg Publishing Office.

Coiro, M. J. (2017). *College students coping with interpersonal stress: Examining a control-based model of coping* (p. 11).

Cramer, P. (2008). Seven pillars of defense mechanism theory. *Social and Personality Psychology Compass, 2*, 1963–1981. doi:10.1111/j.1751-9004.2008.00135

Crane, M. F., Searle, B. J., Kangas, M., & Nwiran, Y. (2018). How resilience is strengthened by exposure to stressors: The systematic self-reflection model of resilience strengthening. *Anxiety, Stress, & Coping,* 1–17. https://doi.org/10.1080/10615806.2018.1506640

de Terte, I., Stephens, C., & Huddleston, L. (2014). The development of a three part model of psychological resilience: Three part model of psychological resilience. *Stress and Health, 30*(5), 416–424. https://doi.org/10.1002/smi.2625

Deasy, C., Coughlan, B., Pironom, J., Jourdan, D., & Mcnamara, P. M. (2015). Psychological distress and lifestyle of students: Implications for health promotion. *Health Promotion International, 30*(1), 77–87. https://doi.org/10.1093/heapro/dau086

Ehlers, A., & Clark, D. M. (2000). A cognitive model of posttraumatic stress disorder. *Behaviour Research and Therapy, 38*(4), 319–345. https://doi.org/10.1016/S0005-7967(99)00123-0

Enns, J., Holmqvist, M., Wener, P., Halas, G., Rothney, J., Schultz, A., . . . Katz, A. (2016). Mapping interventions that promote mental health in the general population: A scoping review of reviews. *Preventive Medicine, 87*, 70–80. https://doi.org/10.1016/j.ypmed.2016.02.022

Folkman, S., Lazarus, R. S., Gruen, R. J., & DeLongis, A. (1986). Appraisal, coping, health status, and psychological symptoms. *Journal of Personality and Social Psychology, 50*(3), 571–579.

Freire, C., Ferradás, M. D. M., Núñez, J. C., & Valle, A. (2018). Coping flexibility and eudaimonic well-being in university students. *Scandinavian Journal of Psychology, 59*(4), 433–442. https://doi.org/10.1111/sjop.12458

Gilbert, P., & Procter, S. (2006). Compassionate mind training for people with high shame and self-criticism: Overview and pilot study of a group therapy approach. *Clinical Psychology & Psychotherapy, 13*(6), 353–379. https://doi.org/10.1002/cpp.507

Gloria, C. T., & Steinhardt, M. A. (2016). Relationships among positive emotions, coping, resilience and mental health: Positive emotions, resilience and health. *Stress and Health, 32*(2), 145–156. https://doi.org/10.1002/smi.2589

Goh, Y. W., Sawang, S., & Oei, T. P. S. (2010). The revised transactional model (RTM) of occupational stress and coping: An improved process approach. *The Australian and New Zealand Journal of Organisational Psychology, 3*, 13–20. https://doi.org/10.1375/ajop.3.1.13

Hayes, S. C. (2004). Acceptance and commitment therapy, relational frame theory, and the third wave of behavioral and cognitive therapies. *Behavior Therapy, 35*(4), 639–665. https://doi.org/10.1016/S0005-7894(04)80013-3

Lazarus, R. S. (1993). Coping theory and research: Past, present, and future. *Psychosomatic Medicine, 55*(3), 234–247.

Li, L. (2014). High rates of prosecution and conviction in China: The use of passive coping strategies. *International Journal of Law, Crime and Justice, 42*(3), 271–285. https://doi.org/10.1016/j.ijlcj.2014.02.002

Mayordomo, T., Viguer, P., Sales, A., Satorres, E., & Meléndez, J. C. (2016). Resilience and coping as predictors of well-being in adults. *The Journal of Psychology, 150*(7), 809–821. https://doi.org/10.1080/00223980.2016.1203276

McLean, L., Steindl, S. R., & Bambling, M. (2018). Compassion-focused therapy as an intervention for adult survivors of sexual abuse. *Journal of Child Sexual Abuse, 27*(2), 161–175. https://doi.org/10.1080/10538712.2017.1390718

Miceli, M., & Castelfranchi, C. (1998). Denial and its reasoning. *British Journal of Medical Psychology, 71*(2), 139–152. https://doi.org/10.1111/j.2044-8341.1998.tb01375.x

Miceli, M., & Castelfranchi, C. (2001). Acceptance as a positive attitude. *Philosophical Explorations, 4*(2), 112–134. https://doi.org/10.1080/10002001058538711

Montuoro, P., & Lewis, R. (2018). Personal responsibility and behavioral disengagement in innocent bystanders during classroom management events: The moderating effect of teacher aggressive tendencies. *The Journal of Educational Research, 111*(4), 439–445. https://doi.org/10.1080/00220671.2017.1291486

Nassif, Y., & Wells, A. (2014). Attention training reduces intrusive thoughts cued by a narrative of stressful life events: A controlled study: Attention training and intrusive thoughts. *Journal of Clinical Psychology, 70*(6), 510–517. https://doi.org/10.1002/jclp.22047

Neff, K. D. (2016). The self-compassion scale is a valid and theoretically coherent measure of self-compassion. *Mindfulness, 7*(1), 264–274. https://doi.org/10.1007/s12671-015-0479-3

Parlamis, J. D. (2012). Venting as emotion regulation: The influence of venting responses and respondent identity on anger and emotional tone. *International Journal of Conflict Management, 23*(1), 77–96. https://doi.org/10.1108/10444061211199322

Reid, A. M., Garner, L. E., Van Kirk, N., Gironda, C., Krompinger, J. W., Brennan, B. P., . . . Elias, J. A. (2017). How willing are you? Willingness as a predictor of change during treatment of adults with obsessive-compulsive disorder. *Depression and Anxiety, 34*(11), 1057–1064. https://doi.org/10.1002/da.22672

Saunders, D. H., Greig, C. A., & Mead, G. E. (2014). Physical activity and exercise after stroke: Review of multiple meaningful benefits. *Stroke, 45*(12), 3742–3747. https://doi.org/10.1161/STROKEAHA.114.004311

Stahl, B., & Goldstein, E. (2010). *A mindfulness-based stress reduction workbook*. New Harbinger Publications.

Tugade, M. M., & Fredrickson, B. L. (2004). Resilient individuals use positive emotions to bounce back from negative emotional experiences. *Journal of Personality and Social Psychology, 86*(2), 320–333. https://doi.org/10.1037/0022-3514.86.2.320

Wheeler, S., & Lord, L. (1999). Denial: A conceptual analysis. *Archives of Psychiatric Nursing, 13*(6), 311–320. https://doi.org/10.1016/S0883-9417(99)80063-6

APPENDIX A

CLIENT WORKSHEETS FOR PASSIVE COPING MODULE

Session 1

Introduction to coping styles

How to participate well

- To have an open and honest discussion about your current levels of stress and coping
- Willing to explore new strategies to improve coping
- Being committed and diligent with assignments to get the best possible outcome

---

The role of the therapist

- To provide evidence-based information about stress and coping techniques
- To help identify new and functional strategies that are useful and help add to your "toolbox" of how to cope with stress and adversities
- Assist in introducing strategies to increase personal psychological resilience and reduce personal stress

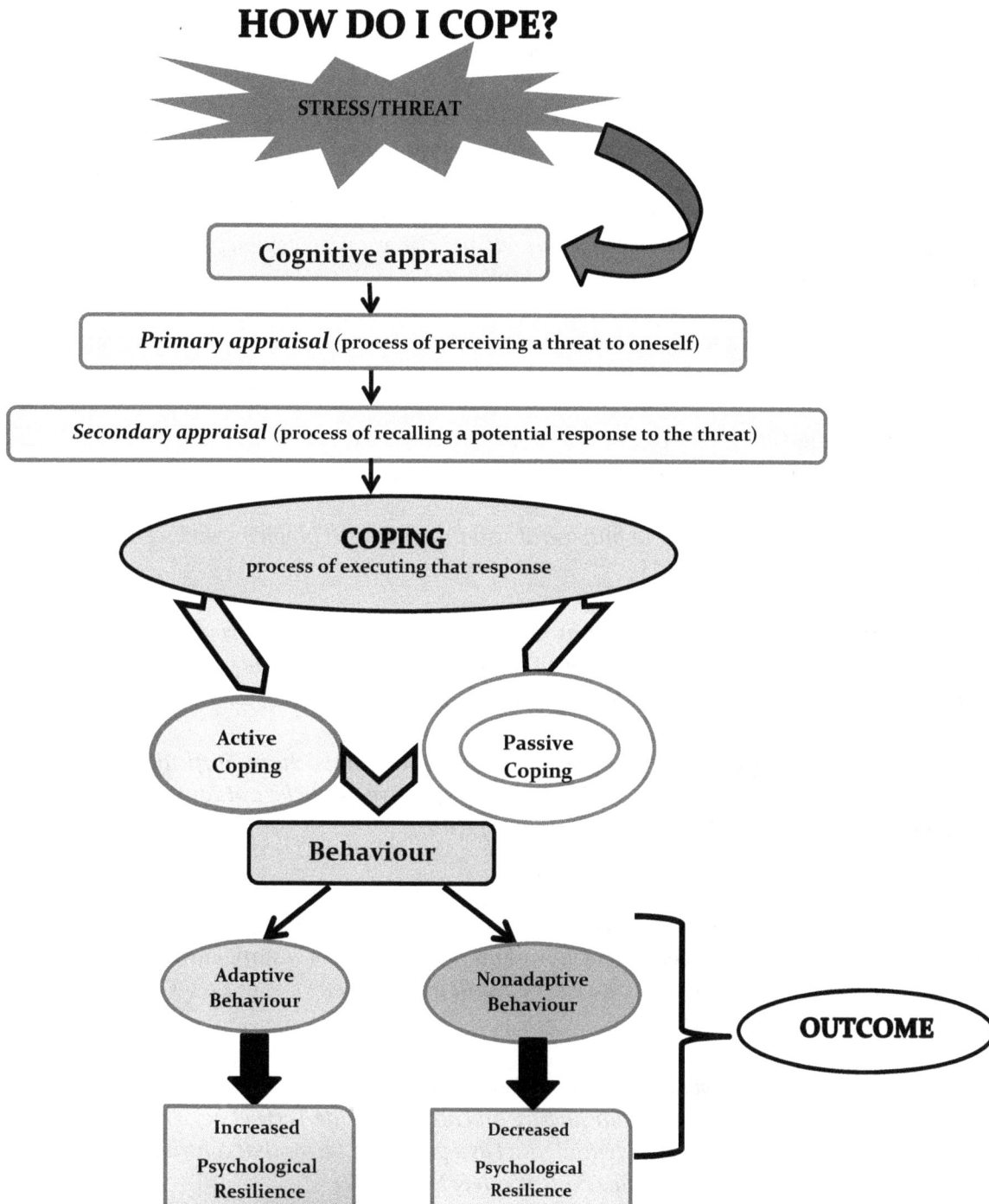

HOW DO I COPE?

STRESS/THREAT

Cognitive appraisal

Primary appraisal (process of perceiving a threat to oneself)

Secondary appraisal (process of recalling a potential response to the threat)

COPING
process of executing that response

Active Coping

Passive Coping

Behaviour

Adaptive Behaviour

Nonadaptive Behaviour

OUTCOME

Increased Psychological Resilience

Decreased Psychological Resilience

Figure A1.1 Modified operational model of stress and coping (passive coping)

Note: *Adapted from "The Revised Transactional Model (RTM) of Occupational Stress and Coping: An Improved Process Approach," by Goh, Sawang, & Oei, 2010.* The Australian and New Zealand Journal of Organisational Psychology, 3, 13-20. Copyright 2010 by Yong Goh.

Note to therapist:

Therapist is encouraged to explain the diagram of the modified operational model of stress and coping (Goh et al., 2010) and use it to identify general or specific examples on how clients normally cope.

Therapist will also need to briefly explain the definitions of cognitive appraisal, active and passive coping, adaptive behaviour, and psychological resilience.

Cognitive appraisal is a process in which an individual assesses if an event is vital to their well-being through utilising both primary and secondary cognitive appraisals.

In primary appraisal, the individual evaluates the risks or benefits to their self-esteem or if the well-being of loved ones is at stake. Values, belief about self and the world, goals, and commitments are activated to evaluate the situation perceived as stressful.

The secondary appraisal allows the individual to decide ways to overcome, reduce, or prevent harm or improve the situation (Booth & Neill, 2017; Crane et al., 2018).

The primary appraisal of a perceived threat leads in turn to the secondary appraisal, which activates a coping response to manage the situation (Folkman et al., 1986).

Active coping: Active coping refers to purposeful ways to deal with problems and seek comfort and social support (Barendregt et al., 2015).

Passive coping *strategies are defined as inactive tactics employed to avoid disagreements and conflicts among people or institutions (Li, 2014). Passive coping strategies include behaviours such as denial, mental disengagement, and behavioural disengagement (Blow et al., 2017).*

Adaptive behaviour: Adaptive behaviours are coping strategies utilised during difficult times to maintain well-being (Tugade & Fredrickson, 2004) and are effective psychological constructs in building psychological resilience in individuals (de Terte et al., 2014).

Psychological resilience: Psychological resilience interventions have the potential to be an inoculation effort, teaching individuals to adapt to their daily stressors (Meichenbaum, 1988). Psychological resilience is an interactive concept, contingent to various factors, and not a static trait of an individual. Hence, it provides evidence that resilience can be learnt and is an ongoing process (Calitz & Santana, 2018; de Terte & Stephens, 2014).

Psychological resilience incorporates robust, resilient, multidimensional building constructs such as coping skills, self-efficacy, self-care, social support, and acceptance (de Terte et al., 2014; Hayes, 2004). Psychological resilience also has the potential to act as a protective factor that contributes to resilience building and effective coping (Enns et al., 2016; Booth & Neill, 2017).

Session 1: The psychology of coping and venting

1   Recall a stressful event that required venting (i.e., stress event)

2   What was your behaviour like around the person or situation that caused the venting?

3   In your opinion, was venting useful? Yes/No

4   Was being vigilant about the use of language and reference to describe a venting event useful?

5   How successful was your attempt to reduce blame language?

6   Did you feel that you coped better by being able to manage your reactions?

Table A1.1 Managing venting behaviour

Stressful incident	Venting	Comments
Incident 1	Venting using "blame language"	
Incident 2	Venting **WITHOUT** using "blame language"	

7   Did reducing blame language influence your mood and general well-being? Explain.

Daily mood tracking graph for this week

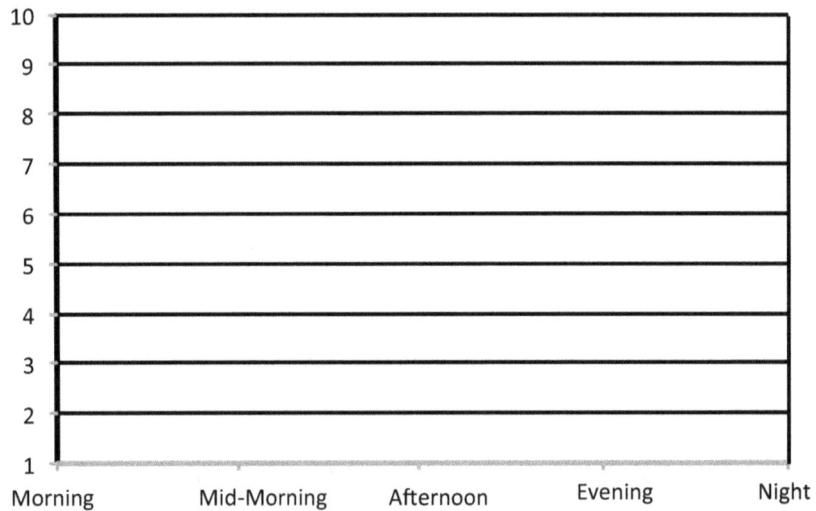

Figure A1.2 Mood tracking graph

Description:

1: Low Mood
10: Elated

CLIENT WORKSHEETS FOR PASSIVE COPING MODULE

SESSION 2

Session 2: Passive coping—Reviewing behaviour disengagement and self-distraction activities

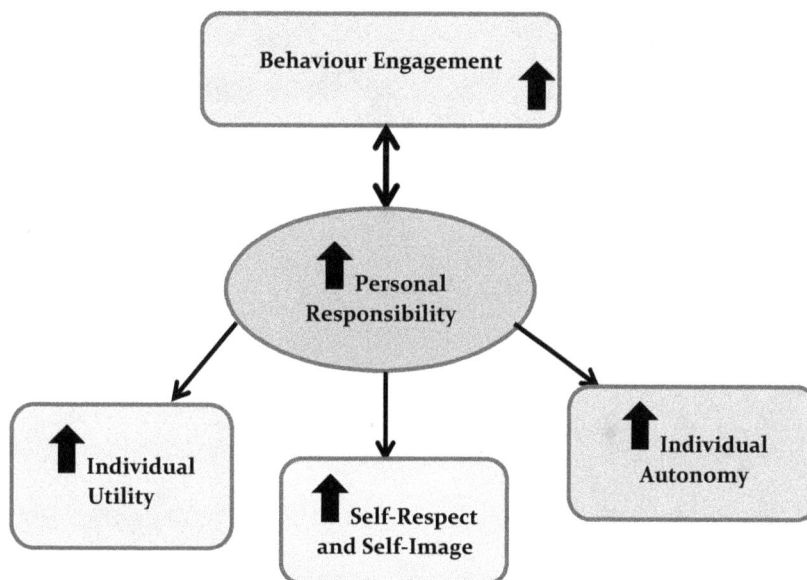

Figure A1.3 Schematic diagram of personal responsibility and behavioural disengagement in innocent bystanders during classroom management events

Note: *Adapted from "Personal responsibility and behavioral disengagement in innocent bystanders during classroom management events: The moderating effect of teacher aggressive tendencies," by Montuoro & Lewis, 2018.* The Journal of Educational Research, 111(4), p. 439–445. Copyright 2018 by Ramon Lewis.

Definitions:

Behaviour disengagement is quitting or withdrawing effort from the attempt to attain the goal.

Self-distraction often occurs when conditions prevent behaviour disengagement.

Self-distraction activities serve to distract an individual or act as an escape strategy.

Examples may include daydreaming, excessive sleeping, watching television, and presumably current distractions such as internet surfing, streaming, and indulging in social media.

---

1   Note any of these behaviours you have engaged in during the last week

Behaviour disengagement

1

2

3

Self-distractions

1

2

3

2   By increasing personal responsibility, both behaviour disengagement and self-distractions can be reduced. Take note on how this is done over the week. How has it impacted the three areas mentioned next?

a   Increase your individual utility

b   Enhance your self-respect and self-image

c   Foster personal autonomy

Planning ahead and being accountable

Here are some action strategies that can further decrease behaviour disengagement and self-distraction:

- Time management
- Skills enhancement
- Reducing distracting activities and behaviours
- Adjusting expectations

Using these suggestions, what can your action strategies be in reducing behaviour disengagement and self-distraction tendencies?

Red flags for behaviour disengagement and self-distractions

Table A1.2 Red flags for behaviour disengagement

Initial warning signs or stress cues	Difficulties in achieving goals (0-10) 0 = No difficulty 10 = Extreme difficulty	Expectations for success (0-10) 0 = Low success 10 = High success

Table A1.3 Handling setbacks

What led to the setback?	My thoughts	My behaviour	What I would do differently?

CLIENT WORKSHEETS FOR PASSIVE COPING MODULE

Session 3

Session 3: Passive coping—Addressing self-blame and denial tendencies

> **Definition:**
>
> Self-blame, a form of passive coping, happens when one excessively criticises and blames oneself.
>
> Denial: Research has shown that individuals use denial as a coping technique when they require more time to digest and monitor a threat before using a more adaptive coping style.

1   Monitor self-blame statements that you used in the last week:

2   What are some of the compassion-focused techniques that you used over the week?

3   Did your mood improve? Yes/No

4   Take note of how your attention, thoughts, behaviours, and language impact your mood

Table A1.4 Tracking attention

Attention
Self-Focus
Others-Focus

Reminder: The alternative is to pay attention to these thoughts and feelings, allowing the self to experience the situation as it is and be nonjudgemental.

Table A1.5 Tracking thoughts

Thoughts
Anticipatory worry thoughts
Mind-reading
Post-analysis

Reminder: The alternative is to distance oneself or use imagery techniques where anxiety-provoking thoughts are replaced by more soothing images or grateful thoughts (i.e., leaves flowing down a stream or thanking the mind for all forms of thoughts and not reacting impulsively).

Table A1.6 Tracking behaviours

Behaviours
Anticipatory worry thoughts
Mind-reading
Post-analysis

Reminder: The alternative is to prioritise values and goals and remind yourself of them during anxiety-provoking activities.

Avoidant behaviours

1

2

3

Language

1

2

3

Reminder: The alternative is to recognise trigger words that increase anxiety and be conscious of the usage and meaning of these words in self-talk and conversations.

4 Did these techniques help? Yes/No

5 Acceptance is an individual's willingness to embrace, rather than tolerate negative or stressful internal experiences during a difficult experience (Charbonneau, 2017; Hayes, 2004). Meanwhile, embracing willingness is not to give in but to embrace unwanted stress or anxiety without trying to inhibit or change these inner experiences.

Was practising acceptance and willingness this week useful? Did it make a difference? How and why?

CLIENT WORKSHEETS FOR PASSIVE COPING MODULE

SESSION 4

Session 4: Metacognition and relapse prevention exercises

Metacognitive Exercise

1   Think about a moderately stressful situation or thought that has been on your mind during the last week.
2   Now, stand up and stretch a little
3   When you are ready, say "10, 9, 8, 7, 6, 5, 4, 3, 2, 1" or "Change"
4   Then quickly write down a **solution-focused action** specific to that intrusive thought (i.e., stop fiddling with the phone, read the first line of the journal article, write a positive statement, get out of bed, get to the gym, or call a friend)
5   Reflect: You now have a plan of action in your hands, which is that to cope, you can either:
    • **Apply** (i.e., activities that bring improvement or resolution to the problem); or
    • **Avoid** (i.e., activities that might delay the discomfort for a while, but maintain the problem)

Recap:

•   Recognise or acknowledge the negative thought
•   Count down 10, 9, 8, 7, 6, 5, 4, 3, 2, 1 or "Change"
•   Replace with an adaptive thought or action

This relapse prevention planning exercise is not just about encouraging one to attempt the worksheets that are made available but instead simply to get back on track as soon as possible.

•   Give yourself time and do not try to force it
•   Make regular practice of your goals and avoid judging your efforts too strenuously

My setback prevention plan (relative to topics discussed in Module 1)

I My self-talk:

1

2

3

4

5

II *How I choose to cope*

1

2

3

III *How will my life change if I have a setback?*

1

2

3

IV *My action plans*

1

2

3

Bibliography

Barendregt, C. S., Van der Laan, A. M., Bongers, I. L., & Van Nieuwenhuizen, C. (2015). Adolescents in secure residential care: The role of active and passive coping on general well-being and self-esteem. *European Child & Adolescent Psychiatry, 24*(7), 845–854. https://doi.org/10.1007/s00787-014-0629-5

Blow, A. J., Bowles, R. P., Farero, A., Subramaniam, S., Lappan, S., Nichols, E., & Guty, D. (2017). Couples coping through deployment: Findings from a sample of national guard families. *Journal of Clinical Psychology, 73*(12), 1753–1767. https://doi.org/10.1002/jclp.22487

Booth, J. W., & Neill, J. T. (2017). Coping strategies and the development of psychological resilience. *Journal of Outdoor and Environmental Education, 20*(1), 47–54.

Calitz, C., & Santana, A. (2018). The art of health promotion: Linking research to practice. *American Journal of Health Promotion, 32*(3), 821–822. https://doi.org/10.1177/0890117118756180

Crane, M. F., Searle, B. J., Kangas, M., & Nwiran, Y. (2018). How resilience is strengthened by exposure to stressors: The systematic self-reflection model of resilience strengthening. *Anxiety, Stress, & Coping,* 1–17. https://doi.org/10.1080/10615806.2018.1506640

de Terte, I., & Stephens, C. (2014). Psychological resilience of workers in high-risk occupations: Guest editorial. *Stress and Health, 30*(5), 353–355. https://doi.org/10.1002/smi.2627

de Terte, I., Stephens, C., & Huddleston, L. (2014). The development of a three part model of psychological resilience: Three part model of psychological resilience. *Stress and Health, 30*(5), 416–424. https://doi.org/10.1002/smi.2625

Enns, J., Holmqvist, M., Wener, P., Halas, G., Rothney, J., Schultz, A., . . . Katz, A. (2016). Mapping interventions that promote mental health in the general population: A scoping review of reviews. *Preventive Medicine, 87,* 70–80. https://doi.org/10.1016/j.ypmed.2016.02.022

Folkman, S., Lazarus, R. S., Gruen, R. J., & DeLongis, A. (1986). Appraisal, coping, health status, and psychological symptoms. *Journal of Personality and Social Psychology, 50*(3), 571–579.

Hayes, S. C. (2004). Acceptance and commitment therapy, relational frame theory, and the third wave of behavioral and cognitive therapies. *Behavior Therapy, 35*(4), 639–665. https://doi.org/10.1016/S0005-7894(04)80013-3

Li, L. (2014). High rates of prosecution and conviction in China: The use of passive coping strategies. *International Journal of Law, Crime and Justice, 42*(3), 271–285. https://doi.org/10.1016/j.ijlcj.2014.02.002

Meichenbaum, D. (1988). Stress inoculation training. *The Counselling Psychologist, 16*(1), 69–90.

Tugade, M. M., & Fredrickson, B. L. (2004). Resilient individuals use positive emotions to bounce back from negative emotional experiences. *Journal of Personality and Social Psychology, 86*(2), 320–333. https://doi.org/10.1037/0022-3514.86.2.320

MODULE 2

SELF-CARE BEHAVIOURS

Overview

> The purpose of this four-session module is to educate clients about self-care strategies and help them improve their self-care.

Goals

> The goal is to encourage clients to think about how they can make positive lifestyle changes (e.g., being more mobile and active, better understanding of nutrition, practising mindful awareness, and practising self-compassion and purpose), which contributes to an increase in their general well-being. Common obstacles to effective self-care are then identified and practical solutions are discussed.

Materials needed

> - Module 2: Self-care behaviours
> - Client worksheets: Self-care behaviours

Module overview

The self-care behaviours module introduces clients to sets of adaptive behavioural activities that help them regulate stress responses, reduce stress levels, and increase general well-being.

DOI: 10.4324/9781003256779-3

Session 5: Getting active and proper nutrition—paying attention

- Establishing therapeutic relationship
- Paying attention to activity and nutrition routine
- Benefits of increased activity and better nutrition
- Personal barriers and obstacles

Here, the therapist explores the client's knowledge about exercise and good nutrition. The therapist introduces the client to the benefits of exercise and good nutrition, then discusses practical options and plans to achieve outcomes that are significant to the client. The client is encouraged to discuss possible solutions for obstacles. Recommendations are then provided to ease learning and increase practice.

Session 6: Mindfulness practice—all about thoughts, feelings, and body sensations

- Being aware of one's thoughts, feelings, and body sensations
- Increasing the ability to stay calm and increase awareness of one's thoughts, feelings, and body sensations
- Ability to choose types of thoughts and feelings to guide actions

In this session, the therapist introduces mindfulness and explores the client's perception of this concept. The therapist is advised to clear any existing negative or general assumptions about mindfulness with clients and is encouraged to practise a simple mindfulness exercise (e.g., taking notice of how a pen is used or how meals are prepared, or being aware of the position of the body when sitting or standing) to make it relatable and safe. The client will also be introduced to an informal mindfulness practice log or record. The recommendation is to encourage the client to practise journaling their daily activities, observing their thoughts, feelings, and body sensations. The client is encouraged to be mindful, implement changes in their behaviour surrounding the situation, and observe outcomes.

Session 7: Practising self-compassion techniques

- Acknowledging existing challenges while being kind to oneself
- Positive self-talk
- Normalising failures and challenges
- Permission to feel feelings
- Mindfulness—maintaining a balanced perspective

The therapist is recommended to review activities in sessions 5 and 6 to assess progress. The therapist will then explore with the client another important aspect of self-care: self-compassion. Self-compassion is when an individual is open, in touch, and kind to themselves in times of struggle and adversities (Neff, 2016).

Self-compassion has three interrelated constructs (Neff, 2016):

- Self-kindness, which refers to unconditional acceptance of oneself by being caring and avoiding harsh judgement
- "Common humanity", which is an understanding that our struggles are part of the human experience

- Mindfulness, which is maintaining a balanced perspective when faced with difficulties; it has been articulated as "social support turned inwards"

Clients will be encouraged to practise these self-care behaviours daily to notice a change in their behaviour, stress levels, and well-being.

Session 8: Learning how to relax, managing time, space, and meaning-making activities; revisiting relapse prevention exercises

- Organising daily work
- Creating realistic and manageable schedules
- Seeking harmony
- Maintaining a pleasant and clean living space

In the final session of this module, the therapist explores how the client relaxes, which is a form of self-care. Suggestions are given to prioritise this behaviour where possible in their daily lives. The therapist then explains alternative forms of self-care, which include time and space management. The client is then asked to plan short-term goals for their immediate projects (home, work, or studies). Maintaining a clean space of work or study is another way that clients are encouraged to declutter and reprioritise what is important to them, increasing adaptive behaviour—which subsequently decreases stress and increases well-being. Relapse prevention exercises are incorporated in this session.

Appendix B

Client worksheets for self-care module

Session 5: Introduction

Therapist to client:

- Welcomes and thanks client for attending the session
- Reassures client that their issues matter
- Reassures and normalises emotional distress

Therapist (T): Perhaps the question to begin with is, "What are your thoughts about the benefits of exercising and eating healthy?"

T: Here are some examples.

Table 2.1 Benefits of exercising for physical and mental health

Benefits of exercising (3 times per week)

1   Better cognitive functioning (i.e., better recall memory, higher concentration, improved learning, and better control of behaviour)
(Ludyga et al., 2018)
2   Reduces risk of stroke (Saunders et al., 2014) and dementia
(Trigiani & Hamel, 2017)
3   Improves concentration, mood, and sleep quality
4   Increases energy levels
5   Reduces weight gain
6   Better physical appearance
7   An opportunity to get to know and engage with others
8   Reduces stress and anxiety

Table 2.2 Good nutrition for mental and physical health

Benefits of eating right

1   Better quality of life
2   Reduces risk of diabetes (Jenkins & Jenks, 2017) and cardiovascular health issues (Saunders et al., 2014)
3   Fewer visits to the doctors or hospital
4   Better skin and hair
5   Fewer cravings

T: Which of these benefits matters most?

T: These are common thoughts and aspirations for many. Now to discuss options and realistic plans in achieving these aspirations.

Table 2.3 Typical and nontypical exercise options

Typical exercise options

- Walking
- Running
- Working out at a gym
- Lifting weights
- Swimming
- Hiking
- Aerobics
- Zumba
- Bike riding or exercise bike
- Roller blading, skateboarding, or riding a scooter
- Martial arts
- Dancing
- Yoga
- Skiing
- Surfing
- Riding horses

Nontypical exercise options

- Bike or walk to work
- Take the stairs
- Make multiple trips up the stairs at home
- Brisk walking with friends or family members
- Park your vehicle in a farther-than-usual location and walk more
- Take your dog for a longer walk
- Get off at an earlier bus stop and walk more
- Carrying groceries in a basket instead of using a cart
- Gardening
- Mow the lawn
- Wash your own car instead of taking it to a car wash
- Walk to the local stores or the nearest town instead of driving, ridesharing, or taking a bus

Table 2.4 Important reminders for effective diet and cooking plans

---

Creating effective diet and cooking plans

1 Be mindful with meal plans and cooking techniques
2 Be conscious about fat and carbohydrate intake
3 Cook at home instead of buying food
4 Limit caffeine and sugar intake
5 Increase daily water intake
6 Replace snacks with fruits or other healthier options

T: What are your thoughts on these suggestions? Are there any hesitations or difficulties?

Note to therapist:

Encourage the client to do their best.

T: Now to discuss some common obstacles to exercising and eating healthy.

Common obstacles to exercising and eating right

- "I have heard and seen it all. These types of exercises don't work for me"
- "I have tried every kind of diet fad and plan out there"
- "I do not have any spare time for exercise"
  - Involve your family members, colleagues, or friends and determine the best time of day or week to include a 30-minute workout daily
  - Get up half an hour earlier to exercise
  - Practise nontypical exercises (e.g., taking the stairs or gardening) daily
  - Enlist an exercise buddy/partner to stay accountable—work out with a partner, roommate, or colleague and have a weekly or monthly progress evaluation
- **Expensive gym memberships**
  - Work out at home
  - Look out for discounted memberships or memberships that are on sale on social media
  - Utilise public parks and recreational facilities in community areas
  - Ask your employers or human resources personnel if there are alternative options for employees to use existing or affiliated gyms

T: Perhaps making a personal activity plan may decrease obstacles.

Worksheet: Making a personal plan to increase my activity level

Functional ideas I have for increasing my activity level are:

1

2

3

Obstacles that I anticipate from now through the next six months:

1

2

3

Possible solutions:

1

2

3

T: Other ways include utilising exercise and nutrition smartphone apps to track personal development. Is this a possible option for you?

┌───┐
│   │
│   Track my exercise and nutrition activity apps   │
│   │
│   │
│   │
│   │
└───┘

1   Download smartphone apps (i.e., pedometer, pacer) to keep track of your daily walking activities and calories burnt
2   Monitor daily food intake
3   Encourage traditional tracking activity worksheets
4   Consider weekly reviews with an exercise partner
5   Plan realistic long-term exercise and nutrition goals. These goals should be achievable and indicate a steady progress

T: In the next session, support systems and the importance of being aware of your thoughts, feelings, and body sensations for personal self-care will be explored.

Note to therapist:

- Ask if client needs further clarification
- Encourage client to attempt assignment for this session in Appendix B: Session 5

Ψ Collaborative tasks checklist

- Therapist has inquired about client's knowledge on exercise and good nutrition
- Benefits of exercise and good nutrition recommendations have been discussed
- Therapist discussed practical options and plans to achieve benefits that are significant to the client
- Client has been encouraged to discuss possible solutions for obstacles. Recommendations were provided to ease learning and increase mastery

Session 6: Introduction

Therapist to client:

- Welcomes and thanks client for attending the session
- Reassure client that their issues matter
- Reassures and normalises emotional distress

My thoughts, feelings, and body sensations

Therapist(T): In today's session, discussions include:

- Ways to increase mindfulness about your thoughts, feelings, and body sensations
- Increasing your personal ability to stay calm and increase awareness of your thoughts, feelings, and body sensations
- Being able to choose types of thoughts and feelings to guide your actions

---

Mindfulness

T: Now to explore mindfulness. What are your thoughts about mindfulness?

Therapist notes:

Note to therapist:

To clarify any negative or general assumptions about mindfulness, explain to the client that there two ways of practising mindfulness—formally and informally. Mindfulness is about being present and aware of whatever is happening in the moment. This is done by simply observing without judgment or harsh criticism about oneself.

Formal practice of mindfulness involves purposely getting into positions (i.e., lying down or sitting) and focusing on deep breathing, thoughts, and emotions. Informal practice of mindfulness can include being present and mindful during daily chores such as studying, eating, cooking, doing the laundry, brushing your teeth, walking, or exercising.

T: The three important components of mindfulness are our thoughts, feelings, and body sensations. This session explores ways to incorporate informal mindfulness exercises to reduce daily stress. Simply do a few quick check-ins of your thoughts, feelings, and body sensations.

Think of an activity that you normally do on a daily basis like doing laundry, brushing your teeth or washing dishes and try to keep your attention on the task as you do it, bringing all of your senses to the experience. If you are brushing your teeth, remind yourself that you are brushing your teeth, feel and listen to the bristles of the toothbrush against your teeth and gums, and smell and taste the toothpaste in your mouth. If you are washing the dishes, know that you are washing the dishes and take in the feel and sound of the water, the smell of the soap, and visual details you might normally gloss over, such as the iridescence of the bubbles.

Note: Reprinted from *A Mindfulness-Based Stress Reduction Workbook* by Stahl & Goldstein, 2010, p. 18. New Harbinger Publications. Oakland, CA. Copyright 2010 by the Copyright Clearance Center (CCC) Marketplace.

T: Now to practise a simple, informal mindfulness exercise.

Mindful exercise

For example, write something down on a piece of paper. Mindfulness can be practised by simply taking notice of the activity. Perhaps one can notice how the pen writes, the content of the writing, or how the writing flowed. What are your observations in practising mindfulness?

T: Other ways one can achieve this is by using an informal mindfulness practice record or check-ins.

Table 2.5 Informal mindfulness practice check-ins

Task	Condition	What did you observe?	What did you observe next?	What are you now aware of?
Reading	"I was reading, but I cannot remember what I just read"	Thoughts: "My exams are in 2 weeks" Feeling: Anxious Body: Tightness in my neck	Started focusing on each paragraph and taking short notes	That when one slows down, one is able to understand and remember what one was reading much better

Task	Condition	What did you observe?	What did you observe next?	What are you now aware of?
Having lunch/ dinner with a friend or colleague	"I rushed and ate the food and did not savour or taste my food at all"	Thoughts: "I have so many deadlines at work" Feeling: Anxious and worried Body: Heart palpitations and sweaty palms	Started focusing on the texture, taste, and appearance of the food on my plate	You may have enjoyed your food better by not rushing through your meal. It is also your lunch hour, so it is all right to relax and focus on yourself

Note: Adapted from *A Mindfulness-Based Stress Reduction Workbook* by Stahl & Goldstein, 2010, p. 49. New Harbinger Publications. Oakland, CA. Copyright 2010 by the Copyright Clearance Center (CCC) Marketplace.

T: What are some of the ways one can practise informal mindfulness check-ins at work, at school, or at home?

1

2

3

T: Are there any barriers anticipated? Barriers:

1

2

3

T: What are some of the possible solutions? Possible solutions:

1

2

3

Note to therapist:

Therapist summarises the day's session and asks client if they have any questions. Encourage them to complete assignment in Appendix B: Session 6.

T: In the next session, self-compassion techniques will be discussed.

Ψ Collaborative tasks checklist

- Introduction to the concept of mindfulness was provided
- Client's previous perception of this concept has been explored
- Existing negative or general assumptions about mindfulness have been explored
- Discussed the use of an informal mindfulness practice record

---

Session 7: Introduction

Therapist (T): **How was your week?**

- Was managing stressful situations better this week?
- In your opinion, was applying the techniques and strategies learnt in the previous sessions useful?
- What was most useful, and what was difficult?

Practising self-compassion

T: Today's session will encompass ways in which one can care for oneself. Is self-compassion a familiar term?

Note to therapist:

Self-compassion is when an individual is open, in touch, and kind to themselves in times of struggle and adversities (Neff, 2016).

T: Here are some strategies to build self-compassion, which encompasses self-kindness, common humanity, and mindfulness (Gilbert & Procter, 2006; Neff, 2016).

Self-kindness

Self-kindness refers to unconditional acceptance of oneself by being caring and avoiding harsh judgements.

T: Perhaps start by relaying a difficult incident or challenge in the recent past.

Note to therapist:

Acknowledge what is difficult for clients and their existing challenges and encourage them to practise self-kindness.

T: Practice time: Perhaps think of a few kind statements that can be used during difficult situations. Here are some examples:

"You are not alone, and others have experienced similar struggles."

Practise "**STOP**":

- **S** = Stop
- **T** = Take a breath
- **O** = Observe
- **P** = Proceed

Note: Reprinted from *A Mindfulness-Based Stress Reduction Workbook* by Stahl & Goldstein, 2010, p. 60. New Harbinger Publications. Oakland, CA. Copyright 2010 by the Copyright Clearance Center (CCC) Marketplace.

Common humanity

T: Another way to be more self-compassionate is to understand that imperfections, failures, and challenges are a part of human life. By acknowledging this, the tendency to feel isolated is less likely.
T: Does positive self-talk sound familiar, or have you used it in the past? If yes, how so?
T: Elaborate on some of your experiences using positive self-talk.

Here are some examples:

Positive self-talk

- It is important to observe any negative self-talk that influences behaviour and action. Negative self-talk examples are "It is never going to get better", "I should be happy", and "I must be great at what I do". Instead, apply statements like "It is okay not to be perfect" or "I'm not faulty".

T: Normalising failures and challenges is another form of self-compassion and taking care of oneself and involves acknowledging that failures are a part of the human experience (e.g., "it is normal to fail", "failure is like a reset button, an opportunity to try again", and "small steps add up"). These statements can decrease hopelessness and isolation and increase purpose.

T: Allowing oneself permission to feel feelings is also useful for maintaining self-compassion.

T: What are your thoughts about that?

T: Is it easy to allow yourself to feel emotions?

Note to therapist:

Encourage the client to feel feelings that can facilitate a comforting response (e.g., "What can I do to take care of myself right now?") and to reduce self-blame statements (e.g., "blaming myself is just causing me more suffering").

Mindfulness

T: Mindfulness in the context of self-compassion involves being aware of one's painful experiences in a balanced way that neither ignores and avoids, nor exaggerates, painful thoughts and emotions (Neff, 2016; Stahl & Goldstein, 2010).

T: While it is important to apply and practise self-compassion, it is equally important to avoid being dramatic but be mindfully compassionate. One way of doing this is to write a compassionate letter or note (optional) to oneself every day for one week about a distressing event—without dramatising, just being compassionate.

Table 2.6 Compassionate note, statement to self, or positive self-talk log-ins

COMPASSIONATE NOTE, STATEMENT TO SELF, or POSITIVE SELF-TALK
Day 1
Day 2
Day 3
Day 4

(Continued)

Table 2.6 (Continued)

COMPASSIONATE NOTE, STATEMENT TO SELF, or POSITIVE SELF-TALK
Day 5
Day 6
Day 7

T: In the next session, which is the final session for Module 2, effective relaxation methods are explored.

Note to therapist:

Therapist summarises the day's session and asks client if they have any questions. Encourage them to complete the assignment in Appendix B: Session 7 before the next week.

Ψ Collaborative tasks checklist

- Asked about client's progress since last sessions
- Client has been introduced to another important aspect of self-care (i.e., self-compassion)
- Three interrelated constructs (Gilbert & Procter, 2016; Neff, 2016) have been discussed and explored with client: self-kindness, common humanity, and mindfulness
- Client has been encouraged to practise these self-care behaviours daily to notice a change in their behaviour, stress level, and well-being

---

Session 8: Introduction

Therapist to client:

- Welcomes and thanks client for attending the session
- Discusses client's week (to keep it consistent)
- Introduces the following session

Learning how to relax

Therapist (T): Everyone has their own way to relax. What are your ways of relaxing?

T: Do you feel content with your choice of relaxation methods, or are you perhaps keen to know more?

T: Some other ways of relaxation that can be helpful are:

- Deep relaxation breathing *(teach simple breathing techniques if they are unsure)*
- Reading a book
- Catching up with friends
- Being creative—playing musical instruments, painting, cooking a meal, or trying a new recipe
- Listening to music
- Watching movies
- Window shopping
- Baking, using aromatherapy, scented candles, or lotions

T: What are your opinions on these suggestions?

T: Perhaps try some of these relaxation methods over this week. What are the top 3 options you want to try?

T: Another important factor in self-care is being able to effectively manage time and space.

T: What is your opinion about your time management skills?

T: Managing your time and space at home, work or study is also a form of self-care. Here are some ways to enhance time management skills. Being mindful of:

- **Organising daily work**
  (school projects, work, or housework)
  - Having short-term or daily goals
  - Organising study groups (for students)
  - Getting feedback from a tutor (for students)
  - Performance management dialogues
- **Maintaining a pleasant and clean living space**
  - Removing clutter

- **Managing time effectively**
  - Recognising distractions (time-stealers)
  - Prioritising self-care activities

T: Perhaps keep track of small changes (wins) that you achieved for the week, as a form of self-care.

Table 2.7 Self-care activities—managing time and space

Managing time and space
Day 1
Day 2
Day 3
Day 4
Day 5
Day 6
Day 7

T: Another form of self-care is practising meaning making, which describes levels of insight of individuals' comprehension of the self and the world (McLean & Pratt, 2006; Lawford & Ramey, 2015). Meaning-making activities can act as a redemptive framework that allows individuals to reframe negative experiences to produce positive outcomes and that is generative (Lawford & Ramey, 2015). These activities can help build purpose and personal transformation, which increases general well-being and reduces stress.

T: Perhaps list one stressful event and observe how narration brought about change, purpose, or a positive outcome and reduced stress.

Table 2.8 Meaning-making activities

Stressful event or circumstances	Meaning making (How do you narrate the intended change to yourself?)	Purposeful outcomes or positive consequences
Day 1 *Example: Being told off by supervisor at work, roommate, or family member for being messy or having poor organising skills.*	*"I want and I am ready to have a clean workspace or home environment so I can be more effective, and maybe I can also show my other roommates/coworkers who are in a similar situation how they can turn things around."*	*Mastery—"I feel like I can do this."* *Feelings of accomplishment—* *"I feel like an adult and a role model."*
Day 2		
Day 3		
Day 4		

Stressful event or circumstances	Meaning making (How do you narrate the intended change to yourself?)	Purposeful outcomes or positive consequences
Day 5		
Day 6		
Day 7		

T: Now to discuss relapse prevention planning. These exercises are available not only to encourage one to attempt the worksheets but also to simply get back on track as soon as possible.

- Give yourself time, and do not try to force it
- Make regular practice of your goals, and avoid judging your efforts too strenuously

These exercises are not to judge or meant to be a competition. They provide pivotal information and enable one to discover individual coping levels and increase personal resilience in order to reduce stress. Being cognisant or aware is important if one foresees any problems in carrying out tasks set for oneself and addresses them promptly.

My setback prevention plan (relative to topics discussed in Module 2)

I My self-talk

1

2

3

4

5

II How I choose to cope

1

2

3

III How will my life change if I have a setback?

1

2

3

IV My action plans

1

2

3

Note to therapist:

- Ask if client needs further clarification
- Encourage client to attempt assignment for this session in Appendix B: Session 8

Ψ Collaborative tasks checklist

- Therapist explored ways in which the client relaxes, which is a form of self-care
- Suggestions were given to prioritise this behaviour where possible in their daily lives
- Therapist explained alternative forms of self-care, which include time and space management
- Client was asked to plan short-term goals for their immediate projects (home, work, or studies)
- Relapse prevention exercises were reviewed

Bibliography

Gilbert, P., & Procter, S. (2006). Compassionate mind training for people with high shame and self-criticism: Overview and pilot study of a group therapy approach. *Clinical Psychology & Psychotherapy, 13*(6), 353–379. https://doi.org/10.1002/cpp.507

Jenkins, D. W., & Jenks, A. (2017). Exercise and diabetes: A narrative review. *The Journal of Foot and Ankle Surgery, 56*(5), 968–974. https://doi.org/10.1053/j.jfas.2017.06.019

Lawford, H. L., & Ramey, H. L. (2015). "Now I know I can make a difference": Generativity and activity engagement as predictors of meaning making in adolescents and emerging adults. *Developmental Psychology, 51*(10), 1395–1406. https://doi.org/10.1037/dev0000034

Ludyga, S., Gerber, M., Brand, S., Pühse, U., & Colledge, F. (2018). Effects of aerobic exercise on cognitive performance among young adults in a higher education setting. *Research Quarterly for Exercise and Sport, 89*(2), 164–172. https://doi.org/10.1080/02701367.2018.1438575

McLean, K. C., & Pratt, M. W. (2006). Life's little (and big) lessons: Identity statuses and meaning-making in the turning point narratives of emerging adults. *Developmental Psychology, 42*(4), 714–722. https://doi.org/10.1037/0012-1649.42.4.714

Neff, K. D. (2016). The self-compassion scale is a valid and theoretically coherent measure of self-compassion. *Mindfulness, 7*(1), 264–274. https://doi.org/10.1007/s12671-015-0479-3

Saunders, D. H., Greig, C. A., & Mead, G. E. (2014). Physical activity and exercise after stroke: Review of multiple meaningful benefits. *Stroke, 45*(12), 3742–3747. https://doi.org/10.1161/STROKEAHA.114.004311

Stahl, B., & Goldstein, E. (2010). *A mindfulness-based stress reduction workbook*. New Harbinger Publications.

Trigiani, L. J., & Hamel, E. (2017). An endothelial link between the benefits of physical exercise in dementia. *Journal of Cerebral Blood Flow & Metabolism, 37*(8), 2649–2664. https://doi.org/10.1177/0271678X17714655

APPENDIX B

CLIENT WORKSHEETS FOR SELF-CARE MODULE

SESSION 5

How to participate well

- Have an open and honest discussion about your current levels of self-care behaviours
- Be willing to explore new strategies to improve self-care tendencies
- Be committed and diligent with assignments to get the best possible outcome

---

The role of the therapist

- To provide evidence-based information about self-care techniques
- To help identify new and functional self-care strategies that are useful and help add to your "toolbox" of how to cope with stress and adversities
- Assist in introducing self-care strategies to increase personal psychological resilience and reduce personal stress

Session 5: Getting active and proper nutrition—paying attention

The following strategies are recommended for an active and healthy lifestyle.

Table A2.1 Benefits of exercising for physical and mental health

---

Benefits of exercising (3 times per week)

1   Better cognitive functioning (i.e., better recall memory, higher concentration, improved learning, and better control of behaviour) (Ludyga et al., 2018)
2   Reduces risk of stroke (Saunders et al., 2014) and dementia (Trigiani & Hamel, 2017)
3   Improves concentration, mood, and sleep quality
4   Increases energy levels
5   Reduces weight gain
6   Better physical appearance
7   An opportunity to get to know and engage with others
8   Reduces stress and anxiety

Table A2.2 Good nutrition for mental and physical health

Benefits of eating right

1   Better quality of life
2   Reduces risk of diabetes (Jenkins & Jenks, 2017) and cardiovascular health issues (Saunders et al., 2014)
3   Fewer visits to the doctors or hospital
4   Better skin and hair
5   Fewer cravings

Table A2.4 Important reminders for effective diet and cooking plans

---

Creating effective diet and cooking plans

1   Be mindful with meal plans and cooking techniques
2   Be conscious about fat and carbohydrate intake
3   Cook at home instead of buying food
4   Limit caffeine and sugar intake
5   Increase daily water intake
6   Replace snacks with fruits or other healthier options

> **Worksheet: Making a personal plan—my activity level**

Functional ideas I have for increasing my activity level are:

    1

    2

    3

Obstacles that I anticipate from now through the next six months:

    1

    2

    3

Possible solutions:

    1

    2

    3

Track my exercise and nutrition activity apps

1 Download smartphone apps (i.e., pedometer, pacer) to keep track of your daily walking activities and calories burnt
2 Monitor daily food intake
3 Encourage traditional tracking activity worksheets
4 Consider weekly reviews with an exercise partner
5 Plan realistic long-term exercise and nutrition goals. These goals should be achievable and indicate a steady progress

CLIENT WORKSHEETS FOR SELF-CARE MODULE

Session 6

Session 6: Mindfulness practice—all about thoughts, feelings, and body sensations

Mindfulness is about being fully aware of whatever is happening in the present moment. This is done by simply observing, watching, and examining without judgement. Mindfulness can be practised in two ways: formally and informally.

Formal practice involves intentionally getting into positions, such as sitting, standing, or lying down, and focusing on the breath, bodily sensations, sounds, other senses, or thoughts and emotions. Informal practice involves bringing mindful awareness to daily activities, such as eating, exercising, doing chores, working, or studying.

Think of an activity that you normally do on a daily basis like doing laundry, brushing your teeth or washing dishes and try to keep your attention on the task as you do it, bringing all of your senses to the experience. If you are brushing your teeth, remind yourself that you are brushing your teeth, feel and listen to the bristles of the toothbrush against your teeth and gums, and smell and taste the toothpaste in your mouth. If you are washing the dishes, know that you are washing the dishes and take in the feel and sound of the water, the smell of the soap, and visual details you might normally gloss over, such as the iridescence of the bubbles.

Note: Reprinted from *A Mindfulness-Based Stress Reduction Workbook* by Stahl & Goldstein, 2010, p. 18. New Harbinger Publications. Oakland, CA. Copyright 2010 by the Copyright Clearance Center (CCC) Marketplace.

Other ways one can achieve this is by using an informal mindfulness practice record or check-ins.

Table A2.5 Informal mindfulness practice check-ins

Task	Condition	What did you observe?	What did you observe next?	What are you now aware of?
Reading	"I was reading, but I cannot remember what I just read"	Thoughts: "My exams are in 2 weeks" Feeling: Anxious Body: Tightness in my neck	Started focusing on each paragraph and taking short notes	That when one slows down, one is able to understand and remember what one was reading much better

(Continued)

Table A2.5 (Continued)

Task	Condition	What did you observe?	What did you observe next?	What are you now aware of?
Having lunch/ dinner with a friend or colleague	"I rushed and ate the food and did not savour or taste my food at all"	Thoughts: "I have so many deadlines at work" Feeling: Anxious and worried Body: Heart palpitations and sweaty palms	Started focusing on the texture, taste, and appearance of the food on my plate	You may have enjoyed your food better by not rushing through your meal. It is also your lunch hour, so it is all right to relax and focus on yourself

Note: Adapted from *A Mindfulness-Based Stress Reduction Workbook* by Stahl & Goldstein, 2010, p. 49. New Harbinger Publications. Oakland, CA. Copyright 2010 by the Copyright Clearance Center (CCC) Marketplace.

What are some of the ways one can practise informal mindfulness check-ins at work, at school, or at home?

1

2

3

Barriers:
1

2

3

Possible solutions:
1

2

3

CLIENT WORKSHEETS FOR SELF-CARE MODULE

SESSION 7

Session 7: Practising self-compassion techniques

1 **Practise some self-kindness**
   Practise "**STOP**"

   - **S** = Stop
   - **T** = Take a breath
   - **O** = Observe
   - **P** = Proceed

   Note: Reprinted from *A Mindfulness-Based Stress Reduction Workbook* by Stahl & Goldstein, 2010, p. 60. New Harbinger Publications. Oakland, CA. Copyright 2010 by the Copyright Clearance Center (CCC) Marketplace.

2 **Indulge in some positive self-talk**
   - It is important to observe any negative self-talk that can influence behaviour and action. Negative self-talk examples include "It is never going to get better", "I should be happy", and "I must be great at what I do". Instead, apply positive statements like "It is okay not to be perfect" or "I'm not defective".
3 **Allow yourself permission to feel feelings**
   - Ask yourself questions that help facilitate a comforting response (e.g., "What can I do to take care of myself right now?" or "Blaming myself is just causing me more suffering")
4 **Practise mindfulness**

Table A2.6 Compassionate note, statement to self, or positive self-talk log-ins

COMPASSIONATE NOTE, STATEMENT TO SELF, or POSITIVE SELF-TALK
Day 1
Day 2
Day 3
Day 4
Day 5
Day 6
Day 7

CLIENT WORKSHEETS FOR SELF-CARE MODULE

Session 8

Session 8: Learning how to relax, managing time, space, and meaning-making activities; revisiting relapse prevention exercises

Relaxation techniques

Choose one or more of these techniques to practise over the coming week:

- Deep relaxation breathing
- Reading a book
- Catching up with friends
- Being creative—playing musical instruments, painting, cooking a meal, or trying a new recipe
- Listening to music
- Watching movies
- Window shopping
- Baking, using aromatherapy, scented candles, or lotions

Managing time and space

Managing your time and space at home, at work, or at school is a form of self-care. Being mindful of:

- **Organising daily work**
  (school projects, work, or housework)
  - Having short-term or daily goals
  - Organising study groups (for students)

- Getting feedback from a tutor (for students)
- Performance management dialogues
- **Maintaining a pleasant and clean living space**
  - Removing clutter
- **Managing time effectively**
  - Recognising distractions (time-stealers)
  - Prioritising self-care activities

Keep track of small changes (wins) that you achieved for the week, as a form of self-care.

Table A2.7 Self-care activities—managing time and space

Managing time and space
Day 1
Day 2
Day 3
Day 4
Day 5
Day 6
Day 7

Meaning-making activities

Meaning-making activities can help build purpose and help you better understand stressful situations. Meaning making is a redemptive or restorative framework that allows individuals to reframe negative experiences to produce positive outcomes and that is generative (Lawford & Ramey, 2015). These activities can help build purpose and personal transformation, which increases general well-being and reduces stress.

Practise meaning-making activities

Table A2.8 Meaning-making activities

Stressful event or circumstances	Meaning making (How do you narrate the intended change to yourself?)	Purposeful outcomes or positive consequences
Day 1 Example: Being told off by supervisor at work, roommate, or family member for being messy or having poor organising skills.	"I want and I am ready to have a clean workspace or home environment so I can be more effective, and maybe I can also show my other roommates/coworkers who are in a similar situation how they can turn things around."	Mastery—"I feel like I can do this." Feelings of accomplishment— "I feel like an adult and a role model."
Day 2		
Day 3		
Day 4		
Day 5		
Day 6		
Day 7		

My setback prevention plan (relative to topics discussed in Module 2)

I My self-talk

1

2

3

4

5

II How I choose to cope

1

2

3

III How will my life change if I have a setback?

1

2

3

IV My action plans

1

2

3

Reminder

These exercises are not to judge or meant to be a competition. They provide pivotal information and enable one to discover individual coping levels and increase personal resilience in order to reduce stress. Being cognisant or aware is important if one foresees any problems in carrying out tasks set for oneself and addresses them promptly.

Bibliography

Jenkins, D. W., & Jenks, A. (2017). Exercise and diabetes: A narrative review. *The Journal of Foot and Ankle Surgery*, *56*(5), 968–974. https://doi.org/10.1053/j.jfas.2017.06.019

Lawford, H. L., & Ramey, H. L. (2015). "Now I know I can make a difference": Generativity and activity engagement as predictors of meaning making in adolescents and emerging adults. *Developmental Psychology*, *51*(10), 1395–1406. https://doi.org/10.1037/dev0000034

Ludyga, S., Gerber, M., Brand, S., Pühse, U., & Colledge, F. (2018). Effects of aerobic exercise on cognitive performance among young adults in a higher education setting. *Research Quarterly for Exercise and Sport*, *89*(2), 164–172. https://doi.org/10.1080/02701367.2018.1438575

Saunders, D. H., Greig, C. A., & Mead, G. E. (2014). Physical activity and exercise after stroke: Review of multiple meaningful benefits. *Stroke*, *45*(12), 3742–3747. https://doi.org/10.1161/STROKEAHA.114.004311

Trigiani, L. J., & Hamel, E. (2017). An endothelial link between the benefits of physical exercise in dementia. *Journal of Cerebral Blood Flow & Metabolism*, *37*(8), 2649–2664. https://doi.org/10.1177/0271678X17714655

SOCIAL SUPPORT

Overview

> The purpose of this four-session module is to encourage clients to use social support. Social support is a vital component in stress reduction (Sippel et al., 2015; Hobfoll & Lilly, 1993).

Goals

> The goal is to help clients to:
>
> - Use available social support as a resource to reduce stress
> - To allow constructive discussion on the use of social support to cope and handle stressful experiences
> - To provide strategies and suggestions to improve general well-being

Materials needed

> - Module 3: Social support
> - Client worksheets: Social support

Module overview

The social support module introduces strategies to clients to access and acquire sources of social support available to them in order to reduce stress and increase well-being.

DOI: 10.4324/9781003256779-4

Session 9: Structural and functional social support

- Explore the client's core understanding of social support
- Explain the Conservation of Resources (COR) theory (Hobfoll & Lilly, 1993)
- Introduce the first two types of social support
  - **Structural support** (the extent of social interaction and their networks)
  - **Functional support** (the experience or perception that social interactions have been beneficial)

In this session, the therapist discusses the client's personal definition of social support and its importance to them. The therapist then proceeds to explain the Conservation of Resources (COR) theory (Hobfoll & Lilly, 1993) and its definition of resources. The COR theory posits that stress occurs when resources are threatened or diminished or if there is a lack of gain from invested resources.

Resources are "things that individuals value or that aids them in obtaining that which is valued" (Hobfoll & Lilly, 1993, p. 129). Social support as a resource and its benefits are discussed. Types of social support that are usually available are explored (Sippel et al., 2015). This session will focus on the first two types of social support—structural and functional social support—as strategies to decrease stress and increase general well-being.

Session 10: Emotional social support

- Explore the client's understanding and relevance of emotional social support
  - **Emotional social support** is the behaviour that nurtures feelings of comfort that allow individuals to believe that they are loved and cared for by their support system (i.e., family members, friends, colleagues, and/or significant other)

Here, the therapist explores access and the importance of emotional social support to the client. The client will then be encouraged to fit emotional social support within the COR theory framework and view this form of social support as a resource that they would like to gain. The client will also be encouraged to utilise this social support and observe if it aids in their ability to cope with stressful situations.

Session 11: Instrumental or material social support

- **Instrumental or material social support** consists of physical goods and services that help reduce the burden of the individual

In this session, the therapist discusses the definition and importance of instrumental or material social support to the client. Similarly, the client will be encouraged to fit this social support within the COR theory framework and view this form of social support as a resource. The client will also be encouraged to utilise this social support and observe if their ability to cope with stressful situations improves by accessing this form of social support.

Session 12: Information or cognitive social support and relapse prevention exercises

- **Information or cognitive social support** involves providing information or guidance to individuals who are going through difficulties or crises

In the final session of the social support module, the therapist explains information and cognitive social support and discusses the importance of this support system to the client. The client will be encouraged to reflect on how these types of social support are resources, and then to discuss the benefits of this social support as both a resource and strategy to help reduce stress levels and increase well-being. Relapse prevention exercises are included and are discussed appropriately according to this module.

Appendix C

Client worksheets for social support module

Session 9: Introduction

Therapist to client:

- Welcomes and thanks client for attending the session
- Reassures client that their issues matter
- Reassures and normalises emotional distress

Therapist (T): What is your definition of social support? How important is social support in maintaining your well-being?

Note to therapist: Explore the meaning of social support specific to the client.

T: According to scientific research, social support refers "to a social network's provision of psychological and material; resources intended to benefit an individual's capacity to cope with stress" (Cohen, 2004, p. 676). Resources are defined as "things that individuals value or that aids them in obtaining that which is valued" (Hobfoll & Lilly, 1993, p. 129). Individuals ideally want to obtain, retain, and protect their resources. Research indicates that stress occurs when these resources are threatened or diminished.

T: Perhaps we should begin with defining what social support resources are.

Objects are resources that are vital for survival. **Conditions** are resources that help individuals attain goals or vital conditions such as stability, affection, and status. **Personal characteristics** are valued resources of the self (social competence, self-esteem, and mastery). **Energies** are resources that increase access to objects, conditions, and personal resources (Hobfoll & Lilly, 1993; Goldfarb & Ben-Zur, 2017; Sippel et al., 2015).

Note to therapist:

Table 3.1 helps clinicians better explore the meaning of social support specific to the client and how they interpret them as social support resources. According to Kaniasty (2020), social support is a critical resource that helps individuals cope, even in dire circumstances (i.e., natural disasters). Social support is also known to have both psychological and social protective functions that benefit individuals and communities.

Table 3.1 Conservation of Resources (COR) theory

Objects	Conditions
Transportation and shelter	Seniority, tenure, and good relationship or marriage
Personal characteristics	**Energies**
Social competence, self-esteem, and sense of mastery	Knowledge, money, and insurance

Note: Adapted from "Resource conservation as a strategy for community psychology," by Hobfoll & Lilly, 1993, *Journal of Community Psychology, 21,* pp. 128–148. Copyright 1993 by the Copyright Clearance Center (CCC) Marketplace.

T: In your opinion, are these social support resources important? Do you have any preference between the different areas of resources?

T: In your opinion, does seeking or improving the previously stated resources help reduce stress and increase general well-being?

T: To summarise, _____ (summarise client's answer)

T: In your opinion, is social support a form of personal resource?

T: Now let us look at this schematic diagram of the types of social support.

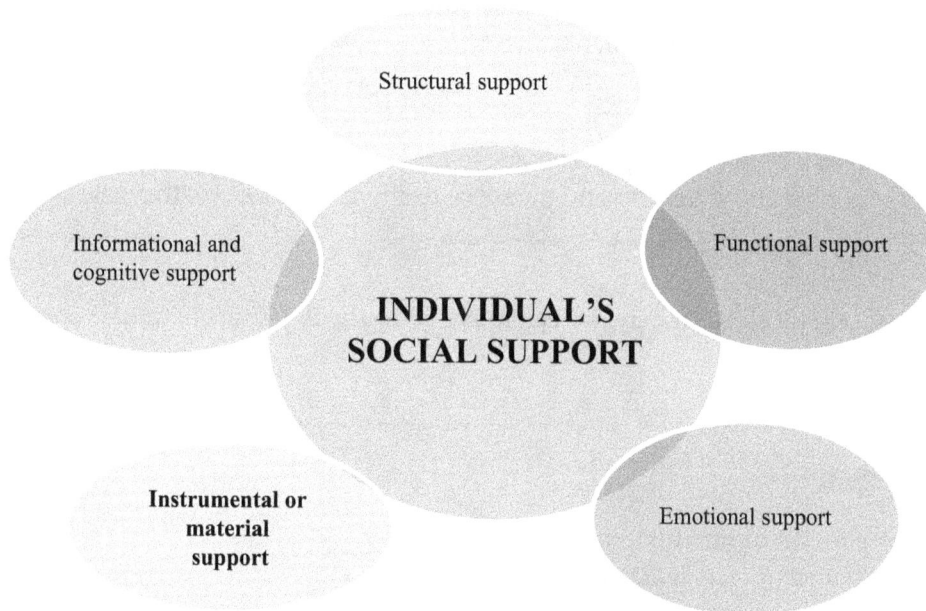

Figure 3.1 Individual's social support

Note: *From "How does social support enhance resilience in the trauma-exposed individual?" by Sippel, Pietrzak, Charney, Mayes, & Southwick, 2015, Ecology and Society, 20(4). Copyright 2015 by Lauren Sippel and Robert Pietrzak.*

T: Scientific research has identified five types of social support:

- **Structural support** is the "size and extent of the individual's social network and the frequency of social interactions" (Sippel et al., 2015, p. 1)
- Structural support is defined as the access of support that can be measured in terms of the regularity (daily, weekly, monthly) and form (face-to-face, telephone, internet) of social interactions (Hwang et al., 2014; Verheijden et al., 2005)
- Structural support is also referred to as social integration (Cohen, 2004)
- **Functional support** is the "experience or perception that social interactions have been beneficial" (Sippel et al., 2015, p. 1)
- **Emotional support** nurtures feelings of comfort that allow individuals to believe that they are loved and cared for by their support system (Sippel et al., 2015, p. 1) (i.e., family members, friends, colleagues, and/or significant others)
- **Instrumental or material support** is "goods and services that help solve practical problems" (Sippel et al., 2015, p. 1)
- **Informational or cognitive support** is an allowance of appropriate materials or services that enables individuals to cope with adversities and adapt to the changes post crisis, usually in a form of guidance (Sippel et al., 2015, p. 1)

T: Is seeking or wanting to improve areas of social support useful in your opinion?

T: Perhaps start by giving some background about what your social support looked like in your younger days (e.g., school, clubs, with your neighbours and community).

T: What was your satisfaction level with the amount of social support then? Perhaps elaborate.

T: Was seeking social support difficult then?

T: How could it have been better?

T: In your opinion, what was the quality of your family members' interactions with their friends, neighbours, and community in general?

T: Perhaps your family's standards or cultural perceptions may have influenced how you sought, gave, or accepted social support. Any thoughts about this?

Note to therapist: Here, attempts are made to explore the cultural ideas, beliefs, and values that the client may hold about persons and the social relationships in which they take part.

T: This is good information. From here, we can move on to the two types of social support that we will discussed today.

Note to therapist:

Recap the definition of structural support with the client.

Structural social support

T: What are your thoughts on the importance of structural social support? In your opinion, is structural social support a beneficial form of social support?

T: Are there any obstacles that can prevent one from receiving this type of support?

T: Perhaps share a recent event in which having structural social support would have been beneficial—maybe during a difficult week at work/home/university.

T: What would your ideal structural social support look like?

T: What is your preference—face-to-face meetings, over the phone, or online?

T: Are there any obstacles to meeting up with these social support resources?

T: Perhaps looking into some strategies that may help reduce or eliminate these obstacles can be helpful.

T: Based on the Conservation of Resources (COR) theory table discussed earlier, are there any particular social support resources that can be obtained by accessing and applying structural social support?

Note to therapist: Recap COR theory table with the client if necessary.

Note to therapist: Use the client's answer in creating a scenario that will provide the client with ways to correct or improve their accessibility to obtain structural social support.

Functional social support

T: Now to discuss another type of social support—functional social support. Functional social support is the experience or perception that social interactions have been beneficial—such as having your social network step in when help is needed (i.e., arranging for transportation to the hospital or work), showing acts of kindness and encouragement, or visiting one when one is ill (Mondesir et al., 2018).

T: Is this type of social support important in your opinion?

T: In the past or even currently, has functional social support been useful to you?

T: Are there any suggestions on how one can increase one's functional social support?

T: Who else may be available to offer this type of social support in times of need?

T: This is excellent! Are there plans to reach out to them?

T: Good idea.

T: Based on the table explained before, where do you think structural social support fits?

T: What are the resources gained or obtained by employing functional social support? (see Table 3.1 COR theory)

Note to therapist: Use the client's answer in creating a scenario that will provide the client with ways to correct or improve their accessibility to obtain functional social support.

T: Perhaps be vigilant this week and allow yourself to access both the structural and functional support systems that we discussed.

T: In the next session, another type of social support—known as emotional social support—will be discussed. Emotional social support is the behaviour that fosters feelings of comfort, leading a person to believe that they are loved, respected, and cared for.

Note to therapist:

Summarise the day's session and ask the client if they have any questions.

Encourage them to complete the assignment in Appendix C: Session 9 before the next session.

Ψ Collaborative tasks checklist

- Client's personal definition of social support and its importance to them were explored
- COR theory (Hobfoll & Lilly, 1993) and its definition of resources were discussed
- Resources were reiterated as "things that individuals value or that aids them in obtaining that which is valued" (Hobfoll & Lilly, 1993)
- Social support (i.e., structural and functional support), as a resource that acts as an adaptive coping strategy and benefits individuals to decrease stress and increase general well-being, was discussed

Session 10: Introduction

Therapist to client:

- Welcomes and thanks client for attending the session
- Reassures client that their issues matter
- Reassures and normalises emotional distress

Therapist (T): How has your week been? Were there any opportunities to access or receive more structural and functional social support?

T: If yes, what was different about the week?

Note to therapist: Reflect on the client's answer to note if there was any reduction in stress levels and increase in general well-being. Focus on the skills mastery that they have achieved by applying this social support.

T: In today's session, the importance of accessing emotional support will be discussed.

Emotional social support

Note to therapist: Emotional support is the behaviour that fosters feelings of comfort, leading a person to believe that they are loved, respected, and cared for.

T: How important is having or accessing emotional social support for you?

Note to therapist: Empathise if appropriate.

T: Perhaps begin by identifying some of the people in your life who offer emotional social support.

T: What is your current level of satisfaction with your emotional social support? Could it be better?

T: What are some of the obstacles that could limit your access to emotional social support?

T: What are some suggestions that may increase the frequency of communicating or meeting up with those who provide you with emotional social support?

T: Are there any other avenues that allow for this social support?

T: It is great that there are other sources who can offer some comfort and care. (Optional)

T: Perhaps recall a time when this support was particularly beneficial in reducing stress.

T: Offering others emotional social support is equally important. What are your thoughts about that?

T: In your opinion, is it comfortable to offer others emotional social support?

T: Based on the COR theory *(Hobfoll & Lilly, 1993),* in what way is emotional social support a resource? *(see Table 3.1 Conservation of Resources (COR) theory)*

T: What are the resources that may be gained by employing this social support?

T: Is there any plan of action to increase your access to this form of support?

T: In the next session, another type of social support—known as instrumental or material support, which are goods and services that help solve practical problems—will be explored.

Note to therapist:

Summarise the day's session and ask client if they have any questions. Encourage them to complete the assignment in Appendix C: Session 10 before the next session.

Ψ Collaborative tasks checklist

- Current access and the importance of emotional social support to the client have been explored
- Client has been encouraged to fit emotional social support within the COR theory framework and view this form of social support as a resource that they would like to gain
- Client has been recommended to utilise this social support and observe if it aids in their ability to cope with stressful situations

Session 11: Introduction

Therapist to client:

- Welcomes and thanks client for attending the session
- Reassures client that their issues matter
- Reassures and normalises emotional distress

Note to therapist: Instrumental or material social support consists of the goods and services that help solve practical problems (Sippel et al., 2015).

Instrumental or material social support

Therapist (T): Perhaps explain the difference it would make if this kind of social support was available.

T: Have you encountered obstacles in attaining this social support currently or in the past?

T: What will it take to achieve this support?

T: Maybe relay a recent event where having instrumental and material support would have been appreciated.

T: What were the obstacles you faced in accessing this type of social support?

T: Now that the obstacles have been identified, are there certain thoughts or behaviours that make it harder to achieve your desired outcome?

Note to therapist: Assist the client in looking at avenues and opportunities that they may have minimised or not attempted that may have contributed to their obstacles.

T: Perhaps it is a good time to reflect on the learning.

T: What would your behaviour look like to better access this type of social support?

T: Imagine how a friend or mentor would respond if they were asked to deal with similar issues.

T: In your opinion, can the original problem be reframed?

T: Based on COR theory *(Hobfoll & Lilly, 1993)*, in what way is instrumental or material support a resource? *(see Table 3.1 COR theory)*

T: By accessing this social support system, do you think it will influence your daily stress levels?

T: Are there any other action plans to increase access to this social support?

T: In the next session, the fifth type of social support—known as informational or cognitive social support—will be explored.

Note to therapist:

Therapist summarises the day's session and asks the client if they have any questions.

Encourage them to complete the assignment in Appendix C: Session 11 before the next session.

Ψ Collaborative tasks checklist

- Therapist discussed the definition and importance of instrumental or material social support with the client
- Client has been encouraged to fit instrumental or material social support within the COR theory framework and view this form of social support as a resource that they would like to gain
- Client has been encouraged to utilise this social support and observe if it aids in their ability to cope with stressful situations

Session 12: Introduction

Therapist to client:

- Welcomes and thanks client for attending the session
- Reassures client that their issues matter
- Reassures and normalises emotional distress

> **Note to therapist:** Informational or cognitive social support is the allowance of appropriate materials or services that enable individuals to cope with adversities and adapt to changes post crisis, usually in the form of guidance (Sippel et al., 2015).

T: Perhaps explain the benefits of having informational or cognitive support.

T: Is this type of social support important currently, or has it been important in the past?

T: Perhaps relay a time when this support was not available. What was your coping technique?

T: In hindsight, were there other ways to cope?

T: Are there any current obstacles that could limit your access in attaining this form of social support?

T: Now that obstacles have been identified, are there any specific behaviours that make it harder to achieve your desired outcome?

> **Note to therapist:** Assist the client in looking at avenues and opportunities that they may have minimised or not attempted that may have contributed to their obstacles.

T: Reflecting on those difficult behaviours, what can be different in increasing access to informational or cognitive social support?

T: Based on the COR theory *(Hobfoll & Lilly, 1993)* (see Table 3.1), how will your resources potentially increase if this social support is utilised?

T: What is your plan of action to increase your access to this form of social support?

T: Perhaps look at how types of social support coping strategies are integrated into relapse prevention planning to reduce stress and increase general well-being.

My setback prevention plan (relative to topics discussed in Module 3)

I My self-talk

1

2

3

4

5

II How I choose to cope

1

2

3

III How will my life change if I have a setback?

1

2

3

IV My action plans

1

2

3

> **Note to therapist:**
>
> Therapist summarises the day's session and asks the client if they have any questions. Encourage them to complete the assignment in Appendix C: Session 12.

Ψ Collaborative tasks checklist

- Therapist has explained the importance of information and cognitive social support system to the client
- Client was invited to reflect on how information and cognitive social support are resources (according to the COR theory) that they would like to gain
- Client has been encouraged to discuss the benefits of this social support as both a resource and strategy to help reduce stress levels and increase well-being
- Relapse prevention planning strategies have been discussed with client

Bibliography

Cohen, S. (2004). Social relationships and health. *American Psychologist, 9*, 676–684.

Goldfarb, R., & Ben-Zur, H. (2017). Resource loss and gain following military reserve duty in Israel: An assessment of conservation of resources (COR) theory. *International Journal of Stress Management, 24*(2), 135–155. https://doi.org/10.1037/str0000036

Hobfoll, S. E., & Lilly, R. S. (1993). Resource conservation as a strategy for community psychology. *Journal of Community Psychology, 21*, 128–148.

Hwang, K. O., Etchegaray, J. M., Sciamanna, C. N., Bernstam, E. V., & Thomas, E. J. (2014). Structural social support predicts functional social support in an online weight loss programme: Structural social support predicts functional social support. *Health Expectations, 17*(3), 345–352. https://doi.org/10.1111/j.1369-7625.2011.00759.x

Kaniasty, K. (2020). Social support, interpersonal, and community dynamics following disasters caused by natural hazards. *Current Opinion in Psychology, 32*, 105–109. https://doi.org/10.1016/j.copsyc.2019.07.026

Mondesir, F. L., Carson, A. P., Durant, R. W., Lewis, M. W., Safford, M. M., & Levitan, E. B. (2018). Association of functional and structural social support with medication adherence among individuals treated for coronary heart disease risk factors: Findings from the Reasons for Geographic and Racial Differences in Stroke (REGARDS) study. *PLoS One, 13*(6), e0198578. https://doi.org/10.1371/journal.pone.0198578

Sippel, L. M., Pietrzak, R. H., Charney, D. S., Mayes, L. C., & Southwick, S. M. (2015). How does social support enhance resilience in the trauma-exposed individual? *Ecology and Society, 20*(4). https://doi.org/10.5751/ES-07832-200410

Verheijden, M. W., Bakx, J. C., van Weel, C., Koelen, M. A., & van Staveren, W. A. (2005). Role of social support in lifestyle-focused weight management interventions. *European Journal of Clinical Nutrition, 59*(S1), S179–S186. https://doi.org/10.1038/sj.ejcn.1602194

APPENDIX C

CLIENT WORKSHEETS FOR SOCIAL SUPPORT MODULE

Sessions 9–12

How to participate well

- Have an open and honest discussion about current levels of social support
- Be willing to explore possible strategies to improve access to various forms of social support
- Be committed and diligent with assignments to get the best possible outcome

---

The role of the therapist

- To provide evidence-based information on the benefits of accessing social support
- To help identify new and functional strategies by accessing social support that is useful and helps add to your "toolbox" of how to cope with stress and adversities
- Assist in introducing strategies for accessing social support to increase personal psychological resilience and reduce personal stress

Sessions 9–12: Types of social support

Social support refers "to a social network's provision of psychological and material; resources intended to benefit an individual's capacity to cope with stress" (Cohen, 2004, p. 676). Resources are defined as "things that individuals value or that aids them in obtaining that which is valued" (Hobfoll & Lilly, 1993, p. 129). Individuals strive to obtain, retain, and protect their resources. Research indicates that stress occurs when resources are threatened or diminished, or when there is a lack of gain.

- Structural support (the extent of social interaction and their networks)
- Functional support (the experience or perception that social interactions have been beneficial in terms of emotional and instrumental needs)
- Emotional support (behaviour that fosters feelings of comfort, leading individuals to believe that they are loved, respected, and cared for by others)
- Material support (physical goods and services that help reduce the burden of the individual)
- Information or cognitive support (providing information or guidance to individuals going through difficulties or crises)

Objects are resources that are needed for survival. Conditions are resources that help individuals attain goals or other valued conditions such as stability, affection, and status. Personal characteristics are valued resources of the self (social competence, self-esteem, and mastery), and energies are resources that increase access to objects, conditions, and personal resources (Hobfoll & Lilly, 1993; Sippel et al., 2015).

Table A3.1 Conservation of Resources (COR) theory

Objects	**Conditions**
Transportation and shelter	Seniority, tenure, and good relationship or marriage
Personal characteristics	**Energies**
Social competence, self-esteem, and sense of mastery	Knowledge, money, and insurance

Note: Adapted from "Resource conservation as a strategy for community psychology," by Hobfoll & Lilly, 1993, *Journal of Community Psychology, 21,* pp. 128–148. Copyright 1993 by the Copyright Clearance Center (CCC) Marketplace.

1   Explain ways in which you have managed to increase access to these types of social support after each of the social support sessions:
- Structural support

- Functional support

- Emotional support

- Material support

- Information or cognitive support

2   How successful has that been?

3   In your opinion, has accessing these forms of social support been useful in reducing personal stress and increasing well-being?

4   Explain how these support systems are now resources:

Types of social support

- Structural support

- Functional support

- Emotional support

- Material support

- Information or cognitive support

<u>My setback prevention plan (relative to topics discussed in Module 3)</u>

I My self-talk:

1

2

3

4

5

II How I choose to cope

1

2

3

III How will my life change if I have a setback?

1

2

3

IV My action plans

1

2

3

> **Reminder:**
>
> These exercises are not to judge or meant to be a competition. They provide pivotal information and enable one to discover individual coping levels and increase personal resilience in order to reduce stress. Being cognisant or aware is important if one foresees any problems in carrying out tasks set for oneself and addresses them promptly.

Bibliography

Cohen, S. (2004). Social relationships and health. *American Psychologist*, 9, 676–684.

Hobfoll, S. E., & Lilly, R. S. (1993). Resource conservation as a strategy for community psychology. *Journal of Community Psychology*, *21*, 128–148.

Sippel, L. M., Pietrzak, R. H., Charney, D. S., Mayes, L. C., & Southwick, S. M. (2015). How does social support enhance resilience in the trauma-exposed individual? *Ecology and Society*, *20*(4). https://doi.org/10.5751/ES-07832-200410

MODULE 4

ACTIVE COPING

Overview

The purpose of this four-session module is to identify active coping strategies. The identification of active coping strategies aims to reduce stress, achieve effective coping, and increase psychological resilience (Eisenbarth, 2019; Gloria & Steinhardt, 2016; Lin, 2016; Sontag-Padilla et al., 2016).

Goals

The goal is to help clients explore existing active coping strategies used to mitigate stress. This module also identifies, expands, and teaches ways to use active coping strategies to increase general well-being and reduce stress.

A supplementary exercise called grateful journaling is included to increase adaptive decision making. In addition, relapse prevention through active coping perspective exercises is incorporated into this session to increase client adherence to learning.

Materials needed

- Module 4: Active coping
- Client worksheets: Active coping

DOI: 10.4324/9781003256779-5

Module overview

The active coping module introduces clients to "purposeful ways to deal with problems" (Barendregt et al., 2015, p. 846). These ways are translated into sets of cognitive and behavioural strategies that will help individuals reframe and react to stress responses effectively. These active coping strategies can reduce stress levels and increase general well-being.

Session 13: Introduction to active coping, stress experience, and reactions

- Introduction to active coping
- Identifying client's cognitive and behavioural reactions to stress
- Overview of stress experiences
- Identification of stages of stress reactions
- Applying active coping and developing effective problem-solving abilities
- In this session, the therapist explores the client's ability to cope with challenges during stressful situations. The therapist then revisits the fundamentals of coping with clients before exploring specific active coping strategies, such as problem-solving techniques. Clients are then introduced to general cognitive and behavioural reactions, and their own reactions are explored. Stages of stress reaction are also identified.

Session 14: Positive reframing, tracking thoughts, behaviour, and learning effective problem-solving techniques

- Revisiting previous week's session
- Positive reframing
- Tracking thoughts, behaviours, and consequences
- Training client to self-monitor thoughts, images, feelings, and behaviours to facilitate adaptive appraisal and effective problem-solving abilities
- Utilising restraint coping to reduce stress

The therapist introduces the concept of reframing and monitoring thoughts, feelings, and behaviours, as well as the importance of restraint coping. These adaptive coping strategies are utilised to reduce stress and enhance psychological well-being and resilience in individuals.

Session 15: Utilising restraint coping, grateful journaling, and relapse prevention exercises

- Exploring how clients have been using coping strategies in past weeks
- Grateful journaling

In this session, clients are introduced to restraint coping, an active coping strategy that assists individuals in dealing with stressors without acting prematurely. While waiting for an appropriate opportunity to react, clients can use restraint coping to take effective measures to manage stress.

A supplementary exercise called grateful journaling, designed to increase adaptive decision making, is also included. Additionally, relapse prevention through active coping perspective exercises is incorporated into this session to increase client adherence to learning.

Session 16: Humour—an active coping strategy

- Revisiting previous week's session
- Humour as active coping, an adaptive coping strategy
- Categories of humour
- Identifying personal types of humour
- Using humour to reframe and solve problems

In the final session of this module, the therapist teaches the client to use humour as an active coping technique. The client identifies their personal humour techniques and uses humour to reframe and solve problems.

Appendix D

Client worksheets for active coping module

Session 13: Introduction

Therapist to client:

- Welcomes and thanks client for attending the session
- Reassures client that their issues matter
- Reassures and normalises emotional distress

Therapist (T): Active coping is defined as "purposeful ways to deal with problems" (Barendregt et al., 2015, p. 846). For most people, it is reflected in the way they view success and failure.

Note to therapist:

The therapist can gently probe the client's undertanding of the term "active coping". This helps the therapist to identify coping mechanisms that the client utilises to solve problems.

Note to therapist:

Therapist is encouraged to explain the diagram of the Modified Operational Model of Stress and Coping (Goh et al., 2010) to review coping methods. Therapist will also need to explain briefly the definitions of cognitive appraisal, active and passive coping, adaptive behaviour, and psychological resilience.

Cognitive appraisal explains a process when an individual assesses if an event is vital to their well-being through utilising both primary and secondary cognitive appraisals.

In primary appraisal, the individual evaluates the risks or benefits to their self-esteem or if the well-being of loved ones is at stake. Belief, values about the self and the world, goals, and commitments are activated to evaluate the situation perceived as stressful.

The secondary appraisal allows the individual to decide ways to overcome, reduce, or prevent harm or to improve the situation (Booth & Neill, 2017; Crane et al., 2018).

The primary appraisal of a perceived threat leads in turn to the secondary appraisal, which activates a coping response to manage the situation (Folkman et al., 1986).

Active coping: Active coping refers to purposeful ways to deal with problems and seek comfort and social support (Barendregt et al., 2015).

Passive coping strategies are defined as inactive tactics employed to avoid disagreements and conflicts among people or institutions (Li, 2014). Passive coping strategies include denial, mental disengagement, and behavioural disengagement (Blow et al., 2017).

Adaptive behaviours are coping strategies utilised during difficult times to maintain well-being (Tugade & Fredrickson, 2004) and are effective psychological constructs in building psychological resilience in individuals (de Terte et al., 2014).

Psychological resilience interventions have the potential to be an inoculation effort, teaching individuals to adapt to their daily stressors (Meichenbaum, 1988). Psychological resilience is an interactive concept, contingent to various factors and not a static trait of an individual. Hence, it provides evidence that resilience can be learnt and is an ongoing process (Calitz & Santana, 2018; de Terte & Stephens, 2014). Psychological resilience incorporates robust, resilient, multi-dimensional building constructs such as coping skills, self-efficacy, self-care, social support, and acceptance (de Terte et al., 2014; Hayes, 2004). Psychological resilience also has the potential to act as protective factor that contributes to resilience building and effective coping (Enns et al., 2016; Booth & Neill, 2017).

T: This diagram may be familiar (see Figure 4.1).

HOW DO I COPE?

STRESS/THREAT

Cognitive appraisal

Primary appraisal (process of perceiving a threat to oneself)

Secondary appraisal (process of recalling a potential response to the threat)

COPING
process of executing that response

Active Coping

Passive Coping

Behaviour

Adaptive Behaviour

Nonadaptive Behaviour

OUTCOME

Increased Psychological Resilience

Decreased Psychological Resilience

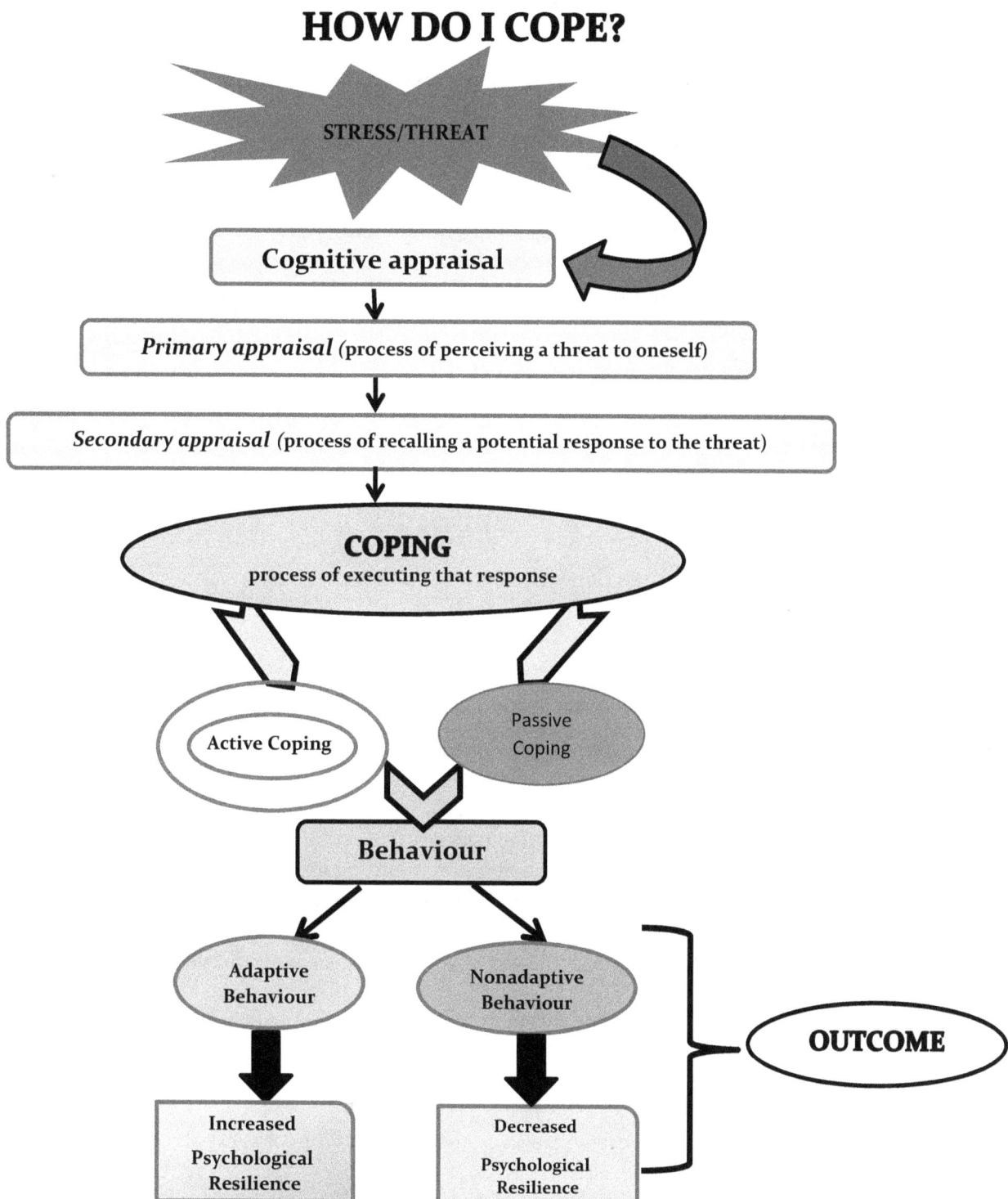

Figure 4.1 Modified operational model of stress and coping (active coping)

Note: *Adapted from* The Revised Transactional Model (RTM) of Occupational Stress and Coping: An Improved Process Approach, *by Goh, Sawang, & Oei, 2010.* The Australian and New Zealand Journal of Organisational Psychology, 3, *13–20. Copyright 2010 by Yong Goh.*

To identify client's cognitive and behavioural reactions to stress

T: Perhaps start with discussing a recent challenge or a stressful experience.
T: In your opinion, how does one define success and failure?
T: In which areas of your life do you feel successful and not as successful?
T: What is common across these situations?

(Explore with the client their confirmatory biases and assumptions)

T: From what I gather, your definition of success is _____, whereas failures are defined as _____.
T: Perhaps your personal definition of success drives your thoughts, behaviours, and actions that are either nonadaptive or adaptive to resolve problems.

Therapist notes:

T: Scientific research has shown that types of stress influence stress experiences and stress tolerance (Bland et al., 2012; Coiro, 2017; Denovan & Macaskill, 2013).
T: Identifying common categories of stress is important in being able to interpret them accurately.
T: Which of these types of stress are your current experiences?
- **Low level stress** (i.e., poor time management, or attending to university assignments)
- **High level stress** (i.e., meeting self and family expectations, relocation or beginning university)
- **Acute stress (short-term)** (i.e., attending a meeting or an interview, or sitting for examinations)
- **Chronic or recurrent stress (long-term)** (i.e., illness, health issues, financial stress, loss of a family member, or family discord)

Note to therapist: Explore the client's views on their current types of stress and clarify if there are tendencies to magnify stress levels.

Therapist notes:

T: Now to explore your general reaction to stress. It is imperative to be cognisant of options that help one react to stress effectively.

T: In your opinion, what is your common reaction to stress? (Therapist shows the diagram to client or reproduces on a whiteboard)

- The individual who gives up or succumbs to the stressful situation and feels defeated; or
- The individual who struggles with the stressful situation; or
- The individual who recovers from the stressful situation back to their prior level of functioning, which is resilience; or
- The individual who does whatever it takes to meet the challenge and grow to an even higher level of functioning and well-being than previously experienced, known as thriving

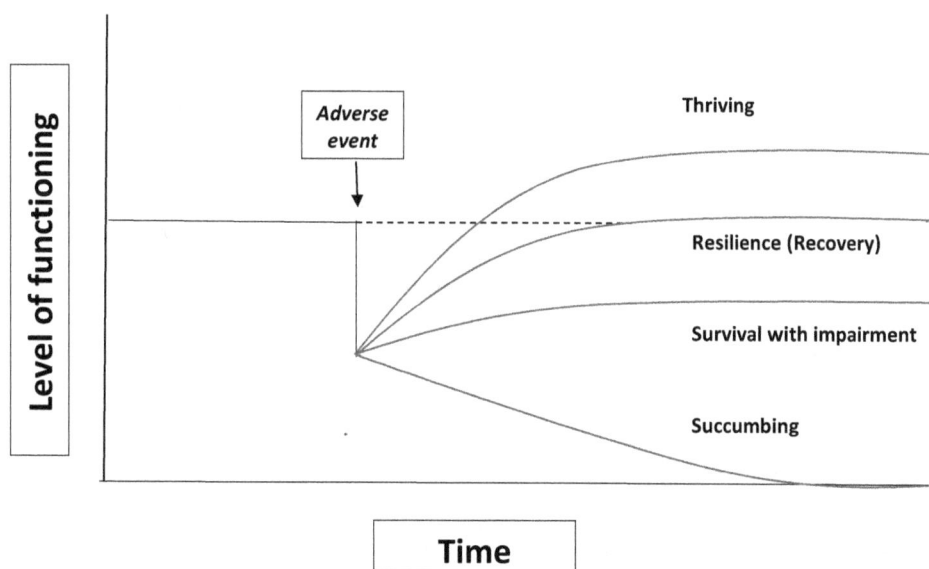

Figure 4.2 Stages of stress reaction

Note: Reprinted from "Potential responses to trauma. Resilience and thriving: Issues, models, and Linkages," *by Carver, 1998.* Journal of Social Issues, *54(2), p.245 -266. Copyright 1998 by the Copyright Clearance Center (CCC) Marketplace.*

Therapist notes:

T: Active coping is reflective of an individual's ability to address distress and increase solution-focused outcomes.

T: When a stressful situation happens, one makes a cognitive decision—or rather, "makes up their mind" or "tells a story to themselves"—on how one wants to react to that stress. This is then accompanied by a reaction or a behaviour that sometimes is adaptive (useful for reducing stress) or nonadaptive (not useful for reducing stress). This influences personal resilience level, which is the ability to adapt to stressful situations and maintain well-being.

T: Going back to the stress example that was just discussed, perhaps explain alternative thoughts and behaviours that you might choose in response to the stressful situation, using the modified operational model of stress and coping (see Figure 4.1) to reframe and solve a problem.

Note to therapist: Explore client's cognitive appraisal of the stressful event using active coping techniques.

Note to therapist:

Observe client's:

1   Automatic, conscious, and identifiable thoughts and images that act as reflex to a situation; often using terms like "should", "ought", or "must" (Meichenbaum, 1988).
2   Confirmatory biases and assumptions becoming schemata (maladaptive core values and behaviour). The more they practise it, the more concrete it becomes.
3   Implicit assumptions that influence decision making and the accompanying behaviour.

T: In your opinion, is the modified operational model of stress and coping useful in identifying your personal coping styles and behaviours that influence outcomes?

T: In the next session, ways to apply adaptive reframing strategy—which is a form of active coping used to reduce stress levels and increase well-being—will be discussed.

Note to therapist:

• Ask if clients need clarification and how they feel after the session

• Briefly summarise and review today's session. Encourage clients to attempt assignment for this session (see Appendix D: Session 13)

Ψ Collaborative tasks checklist

• Therapist explored client's current ability to cope with challenges during stressful situations
• Fundamentals of coping were revisited with clients before exploring specific active coping strategies, such as problem-solving techniques
• Clients were introduced to general cognitive and behavioural reactions, and their own reactions were explored
• Stages of stress reaction were identified

Session 14: Introduction

Therapist inquires about how the client has been in the last week.

- Welcomes and thanks client for attending the session
- Inquires how their week went

T: Over this week, what were your observations on handling stressful situations?
T: Was applying learning from the previous session helpful?

Therapist notes:

T: In the previous session, one's general reaction to stress, and the cognitive and behavioural decisions applied to create opportunities for successful and adaptive outcomes, were identified. In today's session, positive reframing strategies and problem-solving strategies to combat stress are introduced.

Discrete Thought Tracking (DTT) and Action Plan Activity

1.   The situation
Briefly describe the situation that led to your unpleasant feelings

2. Initial thought
What thought first crossed your mind?

3. Rate your mood (0-10)

4. Examine the accuracy of the initial thought

- How successful has this thinking been for you in the past?
- What facts do you have that support or challenge your initial thought?
- What strengths do you have that you may have overlooked?

5. Apply adaptive active coping strategies

6. Rate your mood (0-10)

7. Behavioural changes
Note or observe behavioural changes that were required to make the situation better

8. Action plan
What can you do if this situation arises again?

Knowing your tendencies, how can you better prepare for the situation?

What can you do if you fall back on old habits?

9. Rate your mood (0-10)

Figure 4.3 Discrete thought tracking (DTT) and action plan activity

T: Utilising the DTT, how can you influence a positive change and outcome on a recent stressful or challenging incident?

Therapist notes:

T: It sounds like by applying positive reframing strategies, one can effectively solve problems and make necessary changes that are adaptive.

T: If observed carefully, being aware and selecting the appropriate coping style (step 5 of Figure 4.3) after examining your thoughts may allow for recovery from stressful situations back to your prior level of functioning, which is resilience.

This may influence positive behavioural change that will help reassess your ability to control life events—by looking at the lighter side of life, increasing levels of adaptive coping, and engaging in social support and self-care tendencies.

Note to therapist:

- Ask if the client needs clarification and how they feel after the session
- Briefly summarise and review today's session
- Encourage the client to attempt the assignment for this session (see Appendix D: Session 14)

Ψ Collaborative tasks checklist

- Introduction to thought tracking, behaviours, and consequences was provided to the client
- Client has been encouraged to self-monitor thoughts, images, feelings, and behaviours to facilitate adaptive appraisal and effective problem-solving abilities

Session 15: Introduction

Therapist asks about how the client has been over the last week.

- Welcomes and thanks client for attending the session
- Inquires how their week went

Therapist (T): In this session, restraint coping technique (Corbin et al., 2013) and a supplementary exercise called grateful journaling, along with relapse prevention strategies from an active coping perspective, will be explored.

T: If you recall step 8 (i.e., action plan) from the discrete thought tracking diagram (see Figure 4.3), thoughts and behaviours that increase your awareness about the stressors were discussed. Another way to do this is by practising restraint coping.

Note to therapist:

Recap the discrete thought tracking (DTT) diagram with the client.

Restraint coping is defined as "waiting until an appropriate opportunity to act presents itself, holding oneself back, and not acting prematurely" (Carver et al., 1989, p. 269); this coping strategy encourages individuals to focus on dealing with the stressor at hand.

T: Differing from passive coping, restraint coping involves "taking steps toward managing the stressor rather than ignoring it" (Corbin et al., 2013). The use of restraint coping supports an individual in avoiding nonadaptive behavioural reactions to stress (i.e., alcohol consumption) (Corbin et al., 2013).

T: Is restraint a familiar coping technique?

T: If yes, perhaps relate a situation that required the use of this coping technique (i.e., needed to wait for an appropriate opportunity to react).

T: Was the attempt easy or otherwise?

T: In your opinion, was it beneficial?

T: Moving forward, is applying this strategy comfortable?

T: Do take a look at how one can apply this.

Restraint coping exercises

Table 4.1 Restraint coping exercises

Stress event	Rate initial mood (0-10)	Restraint coping (adaptive reaction)	Rate mood (0-10)
Example: Having a difficult superior or boss	3	Quitting is NOT an option. This may be an excellent opportunity to increase my negotiation skills and learn how to handle confrontation calmly.	6

T: What is your opinion on grateful journaling? While it sounds simple, this activity helps to focus on areas of one's life that are often viewed as minuscule or irrelevant.

> **Note to therapist:**
>
> - Observe if clients are uncomfortable exploring areas in their daily life that they are grateful for
> - If they are, ask them what makes them uncomfortable and offer reasoning on why they feel that way

T: Perhaps consider recording three things that you are grateful for daily for the next week and observe your feelings, thoughts, and behaviours.

T: Now to revisit relapse prevention planning exercises. Just as a reminder, it is not just about encouraging one to attempt the worksheets that are made available but instead to simply get back on track as soon as possible.

- Give yourself time, and do not try to force it
- Make regular practice of your goals and avoid judging your efforts

These exercises are not meant to judge or to be a competition. They are meant to be informative and enable you to discover your individual coping levels and increase personal resilience in order to reduce stress. It is important to be cognisant or aware of any problems in carrying out tasks set for yourself and to address them promptly.

<u>My setback prevention plan (relative to topics discussed in Module 4)</u>

I My self-talk to encourage active coping

1

2

3

4

5

II What are some of the active coping techniques I used that reduced my stress?

1

2

3

III What did I do when I had setbacks?

1

2

3

IV *My action plans to prevent setbacks*

1

2

3

Therapist notes:

Here the therapist discusses obstacles (if any), observations, and progress with the client.

Note to therapist:

- Ask if the client needs clarification and how they feel after the session
- Briefly summarise and review today's session
- Encourage the client to attempt assignment for this session in Appendix D: Session 15

Ψ Collaborative tasks checklist

- Discussed how coping relates to problem solving and introduced restraint coping
- Practised restraint coping exercises
- Introduced supplementary exercise, such as grateful journaling, to increase adaptive decision-making behaviour
- Relapse prevention from an active coping perspective was discussed and incorporated to increase client adherence to learning

Session 16: Introduction

The therapist explores how the client has been in the last week.

- Welcomes client back to the fourth and final session in the active coping module
- Inquires how their week went

Therapist (T): In this final session of the module, another form of active coping—humour—is discussed.

T: Here are some ways that humour is defined in the literature:

- Humour can be learned and practised (Romero & Pescosolido, 2008)
- Humour can be an adaptive coping strategy and may lessen stress (Kuiper & McHale, 2009)
- It can reduce negative emotions and initiate an upward spiral of emotional well-being (Kuiper & McHale, 2009)
- A social lubricant—helps make and maintain friendships and relationships (Romero & Pescosolido, 2008, p. 396; Garrick, 2006)
- Can help lighten the mood and, in the long run, help manage stress better (Martin et al., 2003)
- One has control over the frequency and intensity of daily experience of positive emotions that is received (Romero & Pescosolido, 2008)

T: What is your opinion about humour—is it a teachable skill or rather something that one can observe and learn from others?

T: Humour is categorised into four types (Martin et al., 2003):

- Affiliative (non-hostile jokes, often with friends, which help to build your friendship; "interpersonal rewards")
- Self-enhancing (helps maintain a positive perspective through stress and adversity; "intrapersonal rewards")
- Aggressive (hostile jokes that boost self by criticising others)
- Self-defeating (disparaging humour, a form of confrontation avoidance, when one laughs along with others about their personal weaknesses to gain favour and acceptance)

T: Now being aware of the functions and types of humour, how comfortable are you with using humour during a stressful situation?

T: In the past or even currently, how helpful has humour been in coping with a difficult situation?

Therapist notes:

Identifying personal types of humour

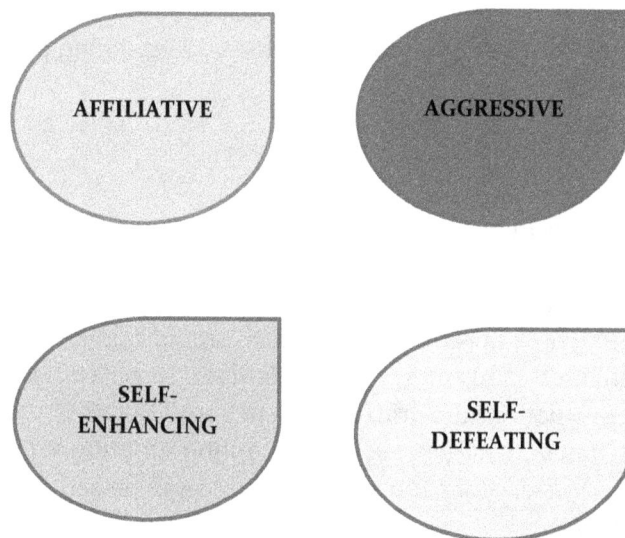

Figure 4.4 Types of humour

Note: *Adapted from "Individual differences in uses of humor and their relation to psychological well-being: Development of the Humor Styles Questionnaire," by Martin, Puhlik-Doris, Larsen, Gray, & Weir (2003).* Journal of Research in Personality, *37(1), 48–75. Copyright 2003 by Rod Martin.*

T: In your opinion, which humour style is most comfortable?
T: Has humour been useful for you?
T: How comfortable are you when people refer to you in their jokes?

Note to therapist:

If client answers "No", then ask how come?

T: Are there any other humour styles that you prefer?
T: Perhaps describe some recent examples.

Note to therapist:

Here, our objective is to shift perspective (encourage client to think of another way to view the stress event) and maintain a humorous outlook on life and to distance the self from negative thoughts.

T: Observe how colleagues, classmates, or family members use humour to cope, get attention, or get out of trouble.

T: Perhaps use humour over the next week (either affiliative or self-enhancing), with the objective of reducing stressful situations.

T: What are some challenges in using humour as a coping strategy?

Note to therapist:

Explore if there are any underlying negative beliefs or assumptions that may be a hindrance in using humour. Encourage repeated practice and observations, which will help improve this coping strategy. If they say "Yes", ask them to explain the understanding around it, then explain the following.

T: By practising humour, it may allow one to reframe or use an alternative way of thinking and behaving when under stress.

T: Are the terms "macabre" and "dark humour" (Fortin & Dupras, 2018) familiar?

T: Scientific research says that dark humour is a common form of humour used among first responders (i.e., police officers, firefighters, and emergency medical services [EMS] personnel) (Fortin & Dupras, 2018)—often used when situations are grim or hopeless and described as the "only way to get by". Individuals exposed to traumatic situations are susceptible to anhedonia (the inability to experience pleasure), and it is necessary for individuals to be open to developing and maintaining a sense of humour (Garrick, 2006).

T: Do you have any experience using dark humour?

T: If yes, in your opinion, how comfortable is using dark humour to cope?

Therapist notes:

T: Now being familiar with the types of humour that are effective, perhaps apply this humour toolkit to reduce stress.

T: To fill up one's humour toolkit, one is recommended to do or reflect on the following:

1 Ask yourself, what is a particular stress that needs to be changed?
2 Apply the humour style that is most comfortable during stressful moments
3 Will it make you feel better afterwards without upsetting others?
4 Tell yourself that having a playful mind is healthy
5 Humour can be therapeutic

6   Ask yourself if others making a joke about you is difficult
7   Allow yourself to apply macabre or dark humour during stressful workdays to cope
8   Ask yourself if you are willing to share jokes with a friend or colleague

---

Note to therapist:

- Ask if the client needs clarification and how they feel after the session
- Briefly summarise and review today's session
- Encourage the client to attempt assignment for this session (see Appendix D: Session 16).

Ψ Collaborative tasks checklist

- Client has been introduced to utilising humour as an active coping technique
- Client identifies their personal humour techniques and uses humour to reframe and solve problems

---

Bibliography

Barendregt, C. S., Van der Laan, A. M., Bongers, I. L., & Van Nieuwenhuizen, C. (2015). Adolescents in secure residential care: The role of active and passive coping on general well-being and self-esteem. *European Child & Adolescent Psychiatry, 24*(7), 845–854. https://doi.org/10.1007/s00787-014-0629-5

Bland, H. W., Melton, B. F., Welle, P., & Bigham, L. (2012). Stress tolerance: New challenges for millennial college students. *College Student Journal, 46*(2), 362–375.

Blow, A. J., Bowles, R. P., Farero, A., Subramaniam, S., Lappan, S., Nichols, E., Guty, D. (2017). Couples coping through deployment: Findings from a sample of national guard families. *Journal of Clinical Psychology, 73*(12), 1753–1767. https://doi.org/10.1002/jclp.22487

Booth, J. W., & Neill, J. T. (2017). Coping strategies and the development of psychological resilience. *Journal of Outdoor and Environmental Education, 20*(1), 47–54.

Calitz, C., & Santana, A. (2018). The art of health promotion: Linking research to practice. *American Journal of Health Promotion, 32*(3), 821–822. https://doi.org/10.1177/0890117118756180

Carver, C. S. (1998). Resilience and thriving. Issues, models and linkages. *Journal of Social Issues, 54*(2), 245–266.

Carver, C. S., Weintraub, J. K., & Scheier, M. F. (1989). Assessing coping strategies: Theoretically based approach. *Journal of Personality and Social Psychology, 56*(2), 267–283.

Coiro, M. J. (2017). *College students coping with interpersonal stress: Examining a control-based model of coping* (p. 11).

Corbin, W. R., Farmer, N. M., & Nolen-Hoekesma, S. (2013). Relations among stress, coping strategies, coping motives, alcohol consumption and related problems: A mediated moderation model. *Addictive Behaviors, 38*(4), 1912–1919. https://doi.org/10.1016/j.addbeh.2012.12.005

Crane, M. F., Searle, B. J., Kangas, M., & Nwiran, Y. (2018). How resilience is strengthened by exposure to stressors: The systematic self-reflection model of resilience strengthening. *Anxiety, Stress, & Coping,* 1–17. https://doi.org/10.1080/10615806.2018.1506640

de Terte, I., & Stephens, C. (2014). Psychological resilience of workers in high-risk occupations: Guest editorial. *Stress and Health, 30*(5), 353–355. https://doi.org/10.1002/smi.2627

de Terte, I., Stephens, C., & Huddleston, L. (2014). The development of a three part model of psychological resilience: Three part model of psychological resilience. *Stress and Health, 30*(5), 416–424. https://doi.org/10.1002/smi.2625

Denovan, A., & Macaskill, A. (2013). An interpretative phenomenological analysis of stress and coping in first year undergraduates. *British Educational Research Journal, 39*(6), 1002–1024. https://doi.org/10.1002/berj.3019

Eisenbarth, C. A. (2019). Coping with stress: Gender differences among college students. *College Student Journal, 53*(2), 151–162.

Enns, J., Holmqvist, M., Wener, P., Halas, G., Rothney, J., Schultz, A., . . . Katz, A. (2016). Mapping interventions that promote mental health in the general population: A scoping review of reviews. *Preventive Medicine, 87,* 70–80. https://doi.org/10.1016/j.ypmed.2016.02.022

Folkman, S., Lazarus, R. S., Gruen, R. J., & DeLongis, A. (1986). Appraisal, coping, health status, and psychological symptoms. *Journal of Personality and Social Psychology, 50*(3), 571–579.

Fortin, A., & Dupras, C. (2018). The macabre humor: An acceptable defense mechanism in critical care? *Canadian Journal of Bioethics* (1). https://doaj.org/article/1f1625fec1954bae82e270cbd6ed94f3

Garrick, J. (2006). The humor of trauma survivors: Its application in a therapeutic milieu. *Journal of Aggression, Maltreatment & Trauma, 12*(1–2), 169–182. https://doi.org/10.1300/J146v12n01_09

Goh, Y. W., Sawang, S., & Oei, T. P. S. (2010). The revised transactional model (RTM) of occupational stress and coping: An improved process approach. *The Australian and New Zealand Journal of Organisational Psychology, 3,* 13–20. https://doi.org/10.1375/ajop.3.1.13

Gloria, C. T., & Steinhardt, M. A. (2016). Relationships among positive emotions, coping, resilience and mental health: Positive emotions, resilience and health. *Stress and Health, 32*(2), 145–156. https://doi.org/10.1002/smi.2589

Hayes, S. C. (2004). Acceptance and commitment therapy, relational frame theory, and the third wave of behavioral and cognitive therapies. *Behavior Therapy, 35*(4), 639–665. https://doi.org/10.1016/S0005-7894(04)80013-3

Kuiper, N. A., & McHale, N. (2009). Humor styles as mediators between self-evaluative standards and psychological well-being. *The Journal of Psychology, 143*(4), 359–376. https://doi.org/10.3200/JRLP.143.4.359-376

Li, L. (2014). High rates of prosecution and conviction in China: The use of passive coping strategies. *International Journal of Law, Crime and Justice, 42*(3), 271–285. https://doi.org/10.1016/j.ijlcj.2014.02.002

Lin, C.-C. (2016). The roles of social support and coping style in the relationship between gratitude and well-being. *Personality and Individual Differences,* 6.

Martin, R. A., Puhlik-Doris, P., Larsen, G., Gray, J., & Weir, K. (2003). Individual differences in uses of humor and their relation to psychological well-being: Development of the humor styles questionnaire. *Journal of Research in Personality, 37*(1), 48–75. https://doi.org/10.1016/S0092-6566(02)00534-2

Meichenbaum, D. (1988). Stress inoculation training. *The Counselling Psychologist, 16*(1), 69–90.

Romero, E., & Pescosolido, A. (2008). Humor and group effectiveness. *Human Relations, 61*(3), 395–418. https://doi.org/10.1177/0018726708088999

Sontag-Padilla, L., Woodbridge, M. W., Mendelsohn, J., D'Amico, E. J., Osilla, K. C., Jaycox, L. H., . . . Stein, B. D. (2016). Factors affecting mental health service utilization among California public college and university students. *Psychiatric Services, 67*(8), 890–897. https://doi.org/10.1176/appi.ps.201500307

Tugade, M. M., & Fredrickson, B. L. (2004). Resilient individuals use positive emotions to bounce back from negative emotional experiences. *Journal of Personality and Social Psychology, 86*(2), 320–333. https://doi.org/10.1037/0022-3514.86.2.320

APPENDIX D

CLIENT WORKSHEETS FOR ACTIVE COPING MODULE

Session 13

How to participate well

- Have an open and honest discussion about your current levels of stress and coping
- Be willing to explore possible strategies to improve active coping
- Be committed and diligent with assignments to get the best possible outcome

---

The role of the therapist

- To provide evidence-based information about stress and active coping techniques
- To help identify new and functional strategies that are useful to you and help add to your "tool-box" of how to cope with stress and adversities
- Assist in introducing active strategies to increase personal psychological resilience and reduce personal stress

HOW DO I COPE?

STRESS/THREAT

Cognitive appraisal

Primary appraisal (process of perceiving a threat to oneself)

Secondary appraisal (process of recalling a potential response to the threat)

COPING
process of executing that response

Active Coping

Passive Coping

Behaviour

Adaptive Behaviour

Nonadaptive Behaviour

OUTCOME

Increased Psychological Resilience

Decreased Psychological Resilience

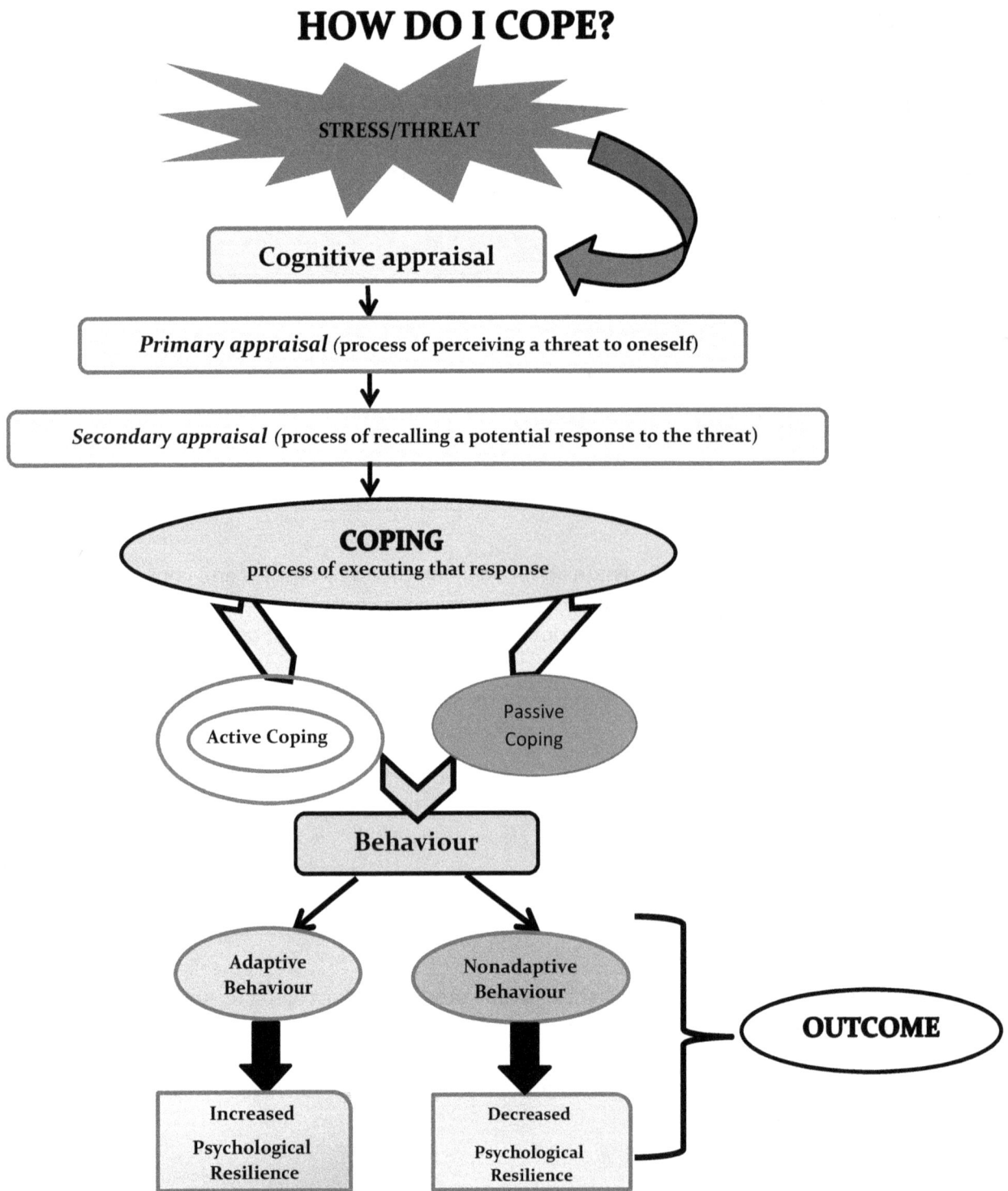

Figure A4.1 Modified operational model of stress and coping (active coping)

Note: *Adapted from "The Revised Transactional Model (RTM) of Occupational Stress and Coping: An Improved Process Approach," by Goh, Sawang, & Oei, 2010. The Australian and New Zealand Journal of Organisational Psychology, 3, 13–20. Copyright 2010 by Yong Goh.*

Definitions:

Cognitive appraisal explains a process when an individual assesses if an event is vital to their well-being through utilising both primary and secondary cognitive appraisals.

In primary appraisal, the individual evaluates risks or benefits to their self-esteem or if the well-being of loved ones is at stake. Belief, values about self and the world, goals, and commitments are activated to evaluate the situation perceived as stressful.

The secondary appraisal allows the individual to decide ways to overcome, reduce, or prevent harm or improve the situation (Booth & Neill, 2017; Crane et al., 2018).

The primary appraisal of a perceived threat leads in turn to the secondary appraisal, which activates a coping response to manage the situation (Folkman et al., 1986).

Active coping: Active coping refers to purposeful ways to deal with problems and seek comfort and social support (Barendregt et al., 2015).

Passive coping strategies are defined as inactive tactics employed to avoid disagreements and conflicts among people or institutions (Li, 2014). Passive coping strategies include denial, mental disengagement, and behavioural disengagement (Blow et al., 2017).

Adaptive behaviours are coping strategies utilised during difficult times to maintain well-being (Tugade & Fredrickson, 2004) and are effective psychological constructs in building psychological resilience in individuals (de Terte et al., 2014). Psychological resilience interventions have the potential to be an inoculation effort, teaching individuals to adapt to their daily stressors (Meichenbaum, 1988). Psychological resilience is an interactive concept, contingent to various factors and not a static trait of an individual. Hence, it provides evidence that resilience can be learnt and is an ongoing process (Calitz & Santana, 2018; de Terte & Stephens, 2014). Psychological resilience incorporates robust, resilient, multidimensional building constructs such as coping skills, self-efficacy, self-care, social support, and acceptance (de Terte et al., 2014; Hayes, 2004).

Psychological resilience also has the potential to act as protective factor that contributes to resilience building and effective coping (Enns et al., 2016; Booth & Neill, 2017).

Session 13: Introduction to active coping, stress experience, and reactions

How do I define "success"?

How do I define "failure"?

In which areas of my life do I feel successful and not as successful?

My current STRESS experience is . . .

- **Single stress occurrence** (i.e., public speaking, or keeping doctor's appointments)
- **Stress event with continuous consequence** (i.e., death of a family member or close friend, or unemployment)
- **Long-term recurrent stress** (i.e., taking examinations)
- **Long-term stress with continuous consequence** (i.e., marital discord, divorce, or serious health conditions)

How do I usually react to stress?

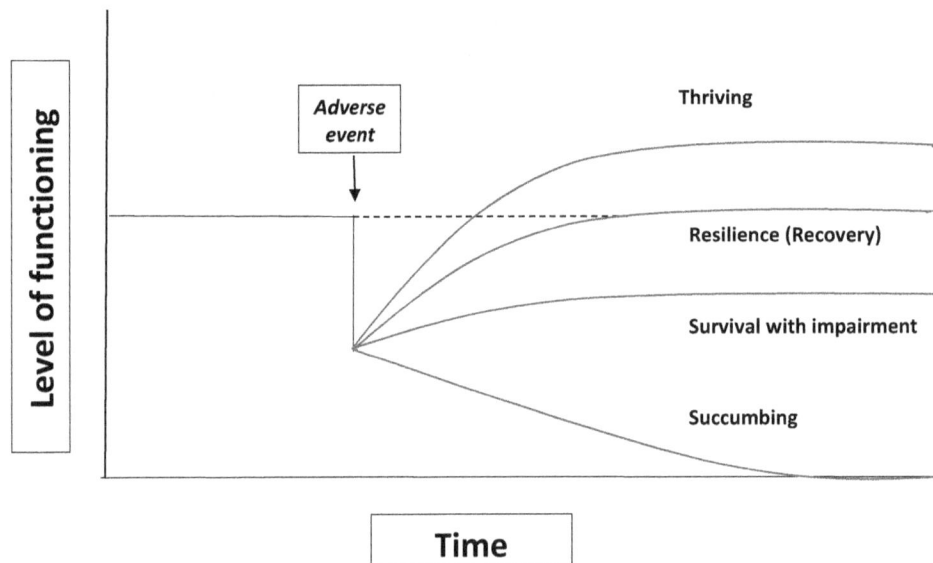

Figure A4.2 Stages of stress reaction

Note: Reprinted from "Potential responses to trauma. Resilience and thriving: Issues, models, and Linkages," by Carver, 1998. Journal of Social Issues, 54(2), p. 245-266. Copyright 1998 by the Copyright Clearance Center (CCC) Marketplace.

- Recall a stressful situation in the recent past
- Monitor the "story" that you tell yourself about the situation
- Observe thoughts and behaviour patterns that were prominent at that time
- Note if these thoughts and behaviour patterns reoccur in other stressful situations
- Note if the same "story" occurs similarly in other stressful situations
- What active coping resources are now available to better solve problems and reduce stress?

CLIENT WORKSHEETS FOR ACTIVE COPING MODULE

SESSION 14:

> **Positive reframing, tracking thoughts, behaviour, and learning effective problem-solving techniques**

Discrete Thought Tracking (DTT) and Action Plan Activity

> **1.   The situation**
> Briefly describe the situation that led to your unpleasant feelings

> **2. Initial thought**
>
> What thought first crossed your mind?

> **3. Rate your mood (0-10)**

> **4. Examine the accuracy of the initial thought**
>
> - How successful has this thinking been for you in the past?
> - What facts do you have that support or challenge your initial thought?
> - What strengths do you have that you may have overlooked?

> **5. Apply adaptive active coping strategies**

> **6. Rate your mood (0-10)**

> **7. Behavioural changes**
>
> Note or observe behavioural changes that were required to make the situation better

> **8. Action plan**
>
> What can you do if this situation arises again?
>
> Knowing your tendencies, how can you better prepare for the situation?
>
> What can you do if you fall back on old habits?

> **9. Rate your mood (0-10)**

Figure A4.3 Discrete thought tracking (DTT) and action plan

1   **Practise: The situation**

2   **Initial thought**

3   **Rate your mood (0-10)**

4   **Examine the accuracy of the initial thought**

5   **Apply adaptive active coping strategies**

6   **Rate your mood (0-10)**

7   **Behavioural change**

8   **Action plan**

9   **Rate your mood (0-10)**

Note to client:

Observe the types of self-talk the client utilises by taking note of words or phrases such as "always", "should", "must", "never", "hopeless", and "can't". Remind yourself: "Catching and interrupting these words may lessen my stress levels."

CLIENT WORKSHEETS FOR ACTIVE COPING MODULE

Session 15: Utilising restraint coping, grateful journaling, and relapse prevention exercises

1   Restraint coping exercises

Table A4.1 Restraint coping exercises

Stress event	Rate initial mood (0-10)	Restraint coping (adaptive reaction)	Rate mood (0-10)
Example: Having a difficult superior or boss	*3*	*Quitting is NOT an option. This may be an excellent opportunity to increase my negotiation skills and learn how to handle confrontation calmly.*	*6*

2 Grateful journaling

Day 1: I am grateful for. . .

1

2

3

Day 2:

1

2

3

Day 3:

    1

    2

    3

Day 4:

    1

    2

    3

Day 5:

    1

    2

    3

Day 6:

    1

    2

    3

Day 7:

    1

    2

    3

<u>My setback prevention plan (relative to topics discussed in Module 4)</u>

I My self-talk to encourage active coping

    1

    2

    3

    4

    5

II What are the active coping techniques that I use to reduce stress?

    1

    2

    3

III What did I do when I had setbacks?

1

2

3

IV My action plans:

1

2

3

Reminder

These exercises are not to judge or meant to be a competition. They provide pivotal information and enable one to discover individual coping levels and increase personal resilience in order to reduce stress. Being cognisant or aware is important if one foresees any problems in carrying out tasks set for oneself and addresses them promptly.

CLIENT WORKSHEETS FOR ACTIVE COPING MODULE

Session 16: Humour—an active coping strategy

- Humour can be learned and practised
- Humour is an adaptive coping strategy; it lessens stress
- It can reduce negative emotions and initiate an upward spiral of emotional well-being
- A social lubricant—helps one make and maintain friendships and relationships
- Can help lighten the mood and, in the long run, help manage stress better
- You have control over the frequency and intensity of daily experience of positive emotions that you receive

Humour is categorised into four types (Martin et al., 2003):

- Affiliative (non-hostile jokes, often with friends, that help build your friendship; "interpersonal rewards")
- Self-enhancing (helps maintain a positive perspective through stress and adversity; "intrapersonal rewards")
- Aggressive (hostile jokes that boost self by criticising others)
- Self-defeating (disparaging humour, a form of confrontation avoidance, when one laughs along with others about their personal weaknesses to gain favour and acceptance)

A shift of perspective (think of another way to view the stress) and maintaining a humorous outlook on life helps distance from negative thoughts.

Recommended types of humour that reduce stress and increase adaptive thoughts and behaviours

---

AFFILIATIVE SELF-ENHANCING

Affiliative humour (non-hostile jokes, often with friends, that help build your friendship; "interpersonal rewards")
Self-enhancing humour (helps maintain a positive perspective through stress and adversity; "intrapersonal rewards")

Humour kit

To fill up one's humour toolkit, one is recommended to do or reflect on the following:

1. Ask yourself, what is a particular stress that needs to be changed?
2. Apply the humour style that is most comfortable during stressful moments
3. Will it make me feel better afterwards without upsetting others?
4. Tell yourself that having a playful mind is healthy
5. Humour can be therapeutic
6. Ask yourself if others making a joke about you is difficult
7. Allow yourself to apply macabre or dark humour during stressful workdays to cope
8. Ask yourself if you are willing to share jokes with a friend or colleague

Bibliography

Barendregt, C. S., Van der Laan, A. M., Bongers, I. L., & Van Nieuwenhuizen, C. (2015). Adolescents in secure residential care: The role of active and passive coping on general well-being and self-esteem. *European Child & Adolescent Psychiatry, 24*(7), 845–854. https://doi.org/10.1007/s00787-014-0629-5

Blow, A. J., Bowles, R. P., Farero, A., Subramaniam, S., Lappan, S., Nichols, E., & Guty, D. (2017). Couples coping through deployment: Findings from a sample of national guard families. *Journal of Clinical Psychology, 73*(12), 1753–1767. https://doi.org/10.1002/jclp.22487

Booth, J. W., & Neill, J. T. (2017). Coping strategies and the development of psychological resilience. *Journal of Outdoor and Environmental Education, 20*(1), 47–54.

Calitz, C., & Santana, A. (2018). The art of health promotion: Linking research to practice. *American Journal of Health Promotion, 32*(3), 821–822. https://doi.org/10.1177/0890117118756180

Crane, M. F., Searle, B. J., Kangas, M., & Nwiran, Y. (2018). How resilience is strengthened by exposure to stressors: The systematic self-reflection model of resilience strengthening. *Anxiety, Stress, & Coping*, 1–17. https://doi.org/10.1080/10615806.2018.1506640

de Terte, I., & Stephens, C. (2014). Psychological resilience of workers in high-risk occupations: Guest editorial. *Stress and Health, 30*(5), 353–355. https://doi.org/10.1002/smi.2627

de Terte, I., Stephens, C., & Huddleston, L. (2014). The development of a three part model of psychological resilience: Three part model of psychological resilience. *Stress and Health, 30*(5), 416–424. https://doi.org/10.1002/smi.2625

Enns, J., Holmqvist, M., Wener, P., Halas, G., Rothney, J., Schultz, A., . . . Katz, A. (2016). Mapping interventions that promote mental health in the general population: A scoping review of reviews. Preventive Medicine, 87, 70–80. https://doi.org/10.1016/j.ypmed.2016.02.022

Folkman, S., Lazarus, R. S., Gruen, R. J., & DeLongis, A. (1986). Appraisal, coping, health status, and psychological symptoms. *Journal of Personality and Social Psychology, 50*(3), 571–579.

Hayes, S. C. (2004). Acceptance and commitment therapy, relational frame theory, and the third wave of behavioral and cognitive therapies. *Behavior Therapy, 35*(4), 639–665. https://doi.org/10.1016/S0005-7894(04)80013-3

Li, L. (2014) High rates of prosecution and conviction in China: The use of passive coping strategies. *International Journal of Law, Crime and Justice, 42*(3), 271–285. https://doi.org/10.1016/j.ijlcj.2014.02.002

Martin, R. A., Puhlik-Doris, P., Larsen, G., Gray, J., & Weir, K. (2003). Individual differences in uses of humor and their relation to psychological well-being: Development of the Humor Styles Questionnaire. *Journal of Research in Personality, 37*(1), 48–75. https://doi.org/10.1016/S0092-6566(02)00534-2

Meichenbaum, D. (1988). Stress inoculation training. *The Counselling Psychologist, 16*(1), 69–90.

Tugade, M. M., & Fredrickson, B. L. (2004). Resilient individuals use positive emotions to bounce back from negative emotional experiences. *Journal of Personality and Social Psychology, 86*(2), 320–333. https://doi.org/10.1037/0022-3514.86.2.320

INDEX

abilities 7, 13, 48, 55, 80, 88, 90, 99, 105–106, 109
acceptance 7, 9, 22–26, 48, 59, 102, 114
accountability 12, 52
action 17–18, 24, 27, 48, 55, 60, 66, 88–89, 91–92, 104, 108, 110, 113
activated 9, 101
active coping 9, 98–116
activities 6–7, 14–19, 21, 24, 27, 47–49, 53, 64
activity 21, 48, 52–53, 56, 108, 111
acute 12
adaptive 7–10, 13, 19, 21–22, 26–27, 47, 49, 86, 98–101, 103–104, 106–109, 111, 113–114
affiliative 115
aggressive 14, 114–115
anhedonia 116
anticipatory 22–23
anxiety 20, 23–25, 27, 50
anxious 22–23, 56–57
appraisal 9, 20, 99, 101, 109
aromatherapy 63
assumptions 48, 55, 58, 104, 106, 116
autonomy 14, 16–17, 19
avoidance 23, 25, 114
avoidant 24
avoidant behaviour 7, 23, 26
awareness 12, 27, 47–48, 55, 110

behavioural 6–9, 13–15, 17–20, 22–24, 26, 47, 89, 91, 99, 101–102, 104, 106–111
behaviour disengagement 7, 14–15, 17–19
blaming language 11–12

capacity 82
checklist 13, 19, 26, 54, 58, 62, 86, 88, 90, 106, 109, 113
circumstances 12–13, 18, 21–22, 64–65, 82
cognisant 28, 65, 105, 111
cognitive 6–7, 9, 13, 20, 23–24, 26, 50, 81, 83, 89, 91, 99, 101, 104–107
cognitive appraisal 7–11, 19, 101, 103, 106
collaborative 13, 19, 26, 54, 58, 62, 86, 88, 90, 106, 109, 113
common humanity 49, 59, 62
compassion 7, 20–21, 26, 48, 61
compassionate 21, 60–62

component 22, 56, 79
concept 7, 9, 25–26, 48, 58, 99, 102
conservation 80, 82, 84–86, 88–89, 91
constructive 79
consumption 110
context 61
contingent 9, 102
conversation 11, 21–22, 24
critical 20, 82
criticism 55
cultivating 26

dark humour 116
daydreaming 14
deadlines 57
decentring 24
declutter 49
definitions 14
dementia 50
denial 7, 9, 19–23, 26, 101
dentifying 115
deployment 27
depression 20
development 18, 53, 115
diabetes 50
disasters 82
discomfort 27
discord 104
discrepancies 22
discrete thought tracking 108, 110
disengagement(s) 9, 13, 14–15, 18, 101
disorders 22
disparaging 114
distraction(s) 7, 13–14, 18–19, 64
distress 8, 25, 50, 55, 82, 87, 89, 91, 101, 105
distressing 61
dysfunctional 27

ecology 83
educational 14
effectively 6–7, 11, 63–64, 99, 105, 109
effort 7, 14, 25, 28, 65, 111
ego 21
emotional 8, 11–12, 20, 25, 50, 55, 82–83, 87, 89, 91, 101, 114

emotional social support 80, 85, 87–88
emotions 12, 23, 56, 61, 114
energy(ies) 50, 82
engagement 14, 17, 25
enhancement 17
esteem 9, 22, 82, 101
evaluation 22, 52

framework 64, 80, 88, 90
frequency 23, 83, 87, 114
functional 21, 27, 52, 83, 85–86
functional social support 80, 85, 87

goals 6–7, 9, 14–19, 21, 24–25, 28, 47, 49, 53, 63, 65,
    82, 98, 101, 111
grateful journaling 98–100, 110–111, 113
guidance 81, 83, 91
gyms 52

habits 108
harmony 49
hindrance 116
hindsight 91
hopelessness 61
hostile 114
humanity 60
humorous 115

imagery 23
impairment 105
impression 16
impulsively 23
inability 20, 116
information 8, 16, 18, 21, 65, 81, 84
informational 83, 89, 91
information or cognitive social support 81
informative 28, 111
inoculation 9, 102
institutions 9, 101
instrumental or material social support 80, 89–90
interaction 11–12, 80, 83–85
interventions 9, 102
intrapersonal 114
intrinsically 15–16
intrusions 27
isolation 22, 61

judgement(s) 48, 55, 59

kindness 85

lifestyle 47

macabre 116
magnify 104
maintenance 18
maladaptive 106
manageable 49
management 14, 17, 19, 49, 63
marital 104
mastery 16, 54, 64, 82, 87

mayordomo 6, 8
meaning making 49, 64
mechanism 20–21, 101
metacognition 6–7, 27
mindful 47–48, 51, 56, 63
mindfulness 48–49, 55–62
modified operational model of stress and coping 6, 8,
    10, 101–106
mood 11–12, 50, 108, 111, 114
mood graph 12
multidimensional 9, 102

nonadaptive 10, 12, 23, 103–104, 106, 110
nonjudgemental 23
nontypical 51–52
normalise 8, 48, 50, 55, 60, 82, 87, 89, 91, 101
nurtures 80, 83
nutrition 47–48, 50, 53–54

obstacles 13, 16–17, 47–48, 51–54, 84, 87, 89, 91, 113
outcome 15–18, 22, 48, 64–65, 89, 91, 105–107, 109

passive coping 6–28, 101, 110
perception 20, 48, 58, 80, 83–85
personality 115
perspective 48–49, 98, 100, 110, 113–115
positive reframing 99, 107, 109
positive self-talk 60–62
postventing 11
prevention 28, 65, 91, 98, 100, 110–113
primary appraisal 9–10, 101, 103
prioritise 24, 49, 64
psychological resilience 6, 8–10, 12, 98, 101–103
psychology 6, 10, 82, 103
psychosomatic 22

reaction 23, 99, 104–107, 110–111
recreational 52
redemptive 64
redirecting 24
reduction 56–57, 60, 79, 87
reenacting 11
reentering 23
reframe 12, 64, 89, 99–100, 106, 116
reframing 24, 99, 106
relapse 18–19, 28, 65, 91, 98, 100, 110–111
relapse prevention exercises 7, 27, 49, 81, 99
relaxation 62–63
resilience 9–10, 28, 65, 83, 99, 102–103, 105–106,
    109, 111
resilient 9, 102
response 6, 9–11, 23, 47, 61, 99, 101, 103, 105–106
restraint 110
restraint coping 99, 110–111, 113
ruminate 12
ruminations 22

savour 57
secondary appraisal 9–10, 101, 103
self-blame 7, 19–21, 26, 61
self-care 49

self-care behaviours 47–66
self-compassion 47–48, 58–62
self-defeating 114
self-distractions 17
self-enhancing 114, 115, 116
self-kindness 48, 59–60, 62
setback 18–19, 28, 65–66, 91–92, 112–113
soothing 21, 23
stressful 7, 9, 11, 13, 21–28, 59, 64–65, 79–80, 88, 90, 99, 101, 104–107, 109, 114, 116
stressor 9, 18, 99, 102, 110
structural 80, 83–87
structural social support 84–85
success 18, 101, 104
succumbing 105

technique 7, 18, 20–23, 26–27, 48, 51, 58–59, 63, 91, 99–100, 106, 110, 112
theory 80, 82, 84–86, 88–91
therapeutic 6, 22, 48, 116

therapist 7–8, 11–22, 24–27, 48–51, 54–55, 58–63, 66, 80–82, 84–91, 99–101, 104–107, 109–111, 113–116
threat 9–10, 20–22, 80, 82, 101, 103
Three-Part Model of Psychological Resilience (3-PR) model 1, 2
toolkit 116
transactional 10, 103
trauma 20, 83, 105, 116

venting 6–7, 11–13
vigilant 16–18, 85
vital 9, 79, 82, 101
void 27

weakness 8, 114
willingness 24–26
withdrawal 14
worksheets 6–7, 28, 47, 49, 53, 65, 79, 81, 98, 100, 111

yoga 51

For Product Safety Concerns and Information please contact our EU
representative GPSR@taylorandfrancis.com
Taylor & Francis Verlag GmbH, Kaufingerstraße 24, 80331 München, Germany